Your Attention Please - Announcer/Cop

Written by:

Dennis R Packer

To my wife, Judy, and children, Brett and Natalie, and grandchildren Jason and Amari Rose to whom I am forever blessed.

Table of Contents

Prologue

I have introduced five presidents, Pope John Paul II, the Queen of England, and the license plates of cars that left their lights on. Public address announcing opened a wide door for me to opportunities and experiences and the chance to meet and work with some of the most exciting people in the world.

The stories you are about to hear are true. The names have been omitted, except for a few, to protect the innocent. Instead, I have paraphrased this noteworthy introduction from the radio and television program "Dragnet," created by Jack Webb, to share with you, the reader, my exploits over the past 50 years in law enforcement and announcing.

I was dubbed "Announcer-Cop" by the news media and officers I worked with. I am very grateful to the many instructors, mentors, fellow partners, civilians, special agents, family members, acquaintances, and even crooks who contributed to my development, confidence, and experiences on and off the sports field and streets. My family, former partners, friends, and colleagues finally convinced me that I needed to put my stories into print.

DENNIS R PACKER

YOUR ATTENTION PLEASE - ANNOUNCER/COP

Chapter 1

The Early Days

From 1965-1968, I was a student at James Monroe High School in North Hills, California. I got my start in announcing in a roundabout way. In high school, I sang in church and school choirs which helped develop my baritone voice. I then joined the Disc Jockey Club at school. The club allowed students to play records during lunch as disc jockeys on the Monroe student radio station KVIK. To become a disc jockey, we had to take a test and apply and receive a Radio Telephone Third Class License from the Federal Communications Commission. Named the "Lord of Sound" for my deep voice, one day, I got in a bit of a jam with the girls' vice principal after playing the Rolling Stones hit, "Let's Spend the Night Together."

From this experience, the Monroe Viking Marching Band instructor, Don Morosic, asked me to announce the band's halftime announcements at home football games. After a few games, Mr. Ben Greene from the athletic department told me about a new sound system installed in the main gym and asked if I could announce the varsity basketball games. Earlier, I had unsuccessfully tried out for the junior varsity basketball team, which turned out to be a good thing. Also, one of the players selected was Doug DeCinces—also a star baseball player—who, after high school, was drafted by Major League Baseball and played for the Baltimore Orioles and California Angels. Years later, I would announce him at Anaheim Stadium.

Figure 1: 1967 Announcing the Monroe Viking Marching
Band at halftime at a home football game.

John Ramsey

I had no prior experience announcing basketball, so I got a ticket
to a Lakers game at the Forum in Inglewood to hear a professional
basketball announcer. I then went to center court and met the
game announcer, John Ramsey. John was famous for announcing
every professional and collegiate team and many other events in
Los Angeles. I introduced myself and asked him for some pointers.
He said knowing the players' names and jersey numbers was the
most important thing. The actions on the court go so fast that an
announcer has to keep up with every play and cannot look down
for a moment.

Figure 2: John Ramsey announced almost every college and professional sports team in Los Angeles from the late 1950s until his passing in 1990.

John got his announcing start at El Camino Junior College in Torrance, CA. He then gave me a copy of a scoresheet he used to record scoring and fouls. I then listened to his announcing techniques, which gave me the skills to announce games.

Varsity basketball coach Bill Rankin was impressed with my announcing ability. After basketball season was over, Monroe Varsity Baseball Coach Denny Holt asked me to announce their home games. I obtained a portable sound system and sat behind home plate and did the scoring and called the game. Monroe third baseman Doug DeCinces called me "John Ramsey Jr" because he said I sounded just like Ramsey. At my high school graduation, my last announcing chore was the invocation.

Los Angeles Valley College

In the fall of 1968, I began studying general education subjects at Los Angeles Valley College in Van Nuys, CA. In addition to attending classes, I announced the Monarch's football, basketball, and baseball, and the pregame and halftime shows at football games for the Monarch Marching Band. I even marched with the band in the Hollywood Lane Christmas Parade, playing the tuba. I graduated with an Associate Arts degree in General Education.

Travels Through Europe

During the summer following my first year at Valley College, I took a trip with the University of Arizona to study urban development in Europe. The course was a whirlwind tour of nine countries, England, France, Belgium, West Germany, Switzerland, Austria, Czechoslovakia, Italy, and Iceland, in 28 days. During five days in Cologne, West Germany, each of us was a guest of a German family. Girls went with daughters, and guys with boys. The coordinator thought I was a girl because of the spelling of my first name. As a result, I had a pink room for the visit. My hosts, Walter and Erika Krieten, and their daughter Gisela had exciting backgrounds.

At 15, Walter became a Luftwaffe pilot during the early years of World War II. During his first flight over England, he was shot down and was a prisoner of war for over four years. He learned to speak English and, after being repatriated back to Germany, taught English and Mathematics as a high school teacher. His wife, Erika, was the daughter of one of the spies for the allies in Cologne during the war. She carried a short-wave radio disguised as luggage. Two Gestapo agents challenged her during her first mission by asking what was in the suitcase. She shamed both agents, saying if you were true German gentlemen, you would not ask what is in my luggage but carry it for a woman. The agents were taken aback and let her go. She showed me her radio and other war items she kept in the basement of her home. The Krieten family resided one block from the famous Cologne Cathedral, which was not bombed during the war. They showed me the tomb of the Three Wise Men in the cathedral.

During the second week of the tour, we crossed the Iron Curtain (still under the control of the Russians) from Austria into Czechoslovakia and visited Prague. Our tour guide was Marcela Lativiscova, a Russian student studying the English language. I developed a friendship with Marcela and asked her out to dinner. I gave her a book about California and an uncirculated Kennedy half-dollar which was a prized souvenir. While walking back to my hotel, two Russian soldiers stopped me. I spoke no Russian, and they did not speak English. I finally made a motion-picture camera gesture with my hands and said I was from Hollywood. They both grinned and repeated, "Hollywood!" I then gave them each a John F. Kennedy half-dollar. They were very appreciative, and one of the soldiers gave me a Lenin medal from his chest. We parted ways, and I made a beeline back to my hotel. I couldn't wait to cross the border from Czechoslovakia into Austria.

While I attended the University of California at Davis, I kept in touch with Marcela by writing letters. Then, one day, the FBI visited me in my dorm room. They wanted to know about my relationship with Marcela because her father was a member of the Supreme Soviet, the highest legislative body of state power in the Union of the Soviet Socialist Republics. I told them we were acquaintances. Their investigation went no further because they thought my letters were pro-USA and not of any concern.

My first trip to Europe whetted my appetite to return the following summer to backpack across Europe. After working half the summer to earn enough money for the trip, a friend, Mark Hawkins, accompanied me on most of the tour. In those days, roundtrip airfare, a Eur-Rail pass, food, and lodging cost under $800. Our first stop was London, where I met Harry, and his wife, Gertrude Wittenbach. Harry was the Canon of Knightsbridge Church in Kensington Gardens, a suburb of London. We were their guests for a couple of days. On the occasion of my marriage, Harry wrote, "Remember Dennis. You are the head of the household as long as you do everything Judy tells you to do."

While riding Deutsche Bahn (German railways) from Cologne to Bonn, I mistakenly got on the wrong train. Eur- Rail passes allowed riders only on 2nd class or "no designated" class trains. I misunderstood the conductor and got on a 1st class train. I was impressed by how nice the 1st class train was. After leaving Cologne station, a different conductor checked tickets in each 1st class cabin. When he got to me, I showed him my Eur-Rail pass. The conductor started yelling at me in German before going to the next compartment. A German businessman told me the conductor acted like a Nazi. He suggested I exit the train as it slowed to enter the Bonn station or face possible arrest. As the train slowed, I jumped off and made my escape. In the background, I could hear a siren coming my way. I felt like I had a part in a World War II movie with the German soldiers closing in on me. I went to a restaurant and ate a long lunch.

Later, I took a train south to Neuberg am Rhein, a municipality along the north bank of the Rhein River and west of Karlsruhe in Southern Germany. The town was the birthplace of Daniel Ertel (1786-1874), a distant relative of Lena Nevill (1876-1952), my father's grandmother. I met a distant cousin, Heinz Degitz, who showed me the Ertel Family Tree on the wall of the Neuberg Rathaus (City Hall). My name was atop the tree. The townspeople were excited by my visit, and we appeared in the Pfalzer Tageblatt newspaper.

Heinz gave us a tour of the countryside along the Rhein River. He showed us a grove of trees, hiding a poignant scene from World War II of a rusting German tank facing a battle-weary American tank. Near the German tank were graves of German soldiers with rifles sticking into the ground and helmets on the butts.

Next, I visited a former Boy Scout buddy stationed at a US Army base near Karlsruhe. Gordon Dunham was assigned to the US Army band and played the trombone. Gordon gave us a tour of the base and the area around Karlsruhe, including a brothel.

After traveling across the Italian Alps to Switzerland, the final leg of my backpacking trip was from Zurich to Paris, France. Unfortunately, I lost my way after leaving the Paris Gare de Lyon train station. To my surprise, an elderly Frenchman asked where I was going and walked several blocks to my destination with me. When I offered to do something for him, for his assistance, he replied, "America saved Paris and France in World War II. Merci beaucoup (thank you very much)."

UC Davis

In September 1970, I transferred from LAVC to the University of California at Davis to further my studies in Political Science and earned a bachelor's degree. I continued sports announcing and did the pregame and halftime shows for the Cal-Aggies Marching Band. The sports I announced included basketball, baseball, swim meets, fencing, synchronized swimming, gymnastics competitions, and sheepdog trials wherein sheepdogs' herd various animals, including sheep, around obstacles into pens.

Bark Like a Dog

The UC Davis football season in 1971 was memorable because the Aggies won nine out of ten games in the last seconds of play. Head Coach Jim Sochor led the Aggies to an overall record of nine wins and one loss, and they shared the Far Western Conference title with Chico State.

At the game at Humboldt State, the Aggies won in the last seconds of play with a field goal kicked by Adrian Wagner. What made it exciting was fog obscured the goalposts. The officials had to stand on ladders to see the ball go through the uprights. Until the officials signaled the field goal was good, the crowd had to wait in nervous expectation.

However, November 6, 1971, at Cal State Hayward was the most exciting game of the year. The Aggies scored 16 points in 20 seconds to defeat Hayward in the "Miracle Game." I assisted in the broadcast and told the radio audience I would end up in the hospital after such an exciting game.

In two days, I will celebrate my 21st birthday in style. One of the guys in my dorm dad worked in a strip joint along the Tenderloin District in San Francisco and arranged a stripper to perform during my birthday celebration.

I went to bed on the eve of my birthday, looking forward to the next day with great anticipation. However, around midnight, I had a horrible stomachache. There was nothing to do to stop the pain. In addition to coming out both ends, the pain in my abdomen intensified. I told my roommate that I felt like I was going to die. At 3 am, I crawled to the Student Health Center across the street from the dorm. Next, the doctor said my white blood count was very high, indicating I would have surgery to remove my appendix. The doctor said they were looking for a surgeon to do the surgery, and they might have to use a veterinarian. I did not care whom they got because the pain was excruciating. Finally, a surgeon arrived and told me he was from the Veterinary School, and the one side effect I would have from the surgery was that I would bark like a dog. He was trying to cheer me up.

I could sign the release to do the surgery because I was 21. I called my parents, and they wished me well. The surgery was a success. While in recovery, I saw several coeds at the foot of my bed. I learned later that a football player was in bed next to me, and they were visiting him.

My dorm buddies came by and told me the birthday party was a success, and the guys in my dorm had a great time with the stripper.

Picnic Day '72

In the fall of 1971, I learned that the radical student government would cancel the annual Picnic Day celebration in April 1972 in favor of Earth Day. Picnic Day, a tradition dating back to 1909, had been the largest student-run event attracting thousands to the university for a weekend, showcasing its students' and faculty's diversity and achievements, and served as an open house.

Unfortunately, the university had only canceled Picnic Day five times because of an outbreak of hoof and mouth disease, construction on campus, and World War II. Picnic Day was worth saving. I led a group of students from Beckett Hall in successfully overturning the student senate and holding the event, including Earth Day activities. I became the event's chairman and sought to bring back the history of UC Davis with a parade, hot air balloon, and events across campus. With Publicity Chairwoman Linda Clingan, we drove to Calistoga, CA, to ask 1916 Davis graduate and Disney artist, Ben Sharpsteen, to use his Briarcliff Lithograph for the 1972 Picnic Day program cover. We also made him the honorary grand marshal of the parade. My brother-in-law and member of Gary Puckett and the Union Gap, Gary "Mutha" Withem, recorded the theme song, "Remember the First Time," which played on the radio to advertise Picnic Day. The event was a memorable experience that cemented Picnic Day for the years to come.

Figure 3: 1972 UC Davis Picnic Day Board of Directors. From left to right: Jean Cain, Judie Lea, Diana Barnes, Rob Lamb, Laura Lockhart, Robert Figari, Jasmin Flores, me with the parted hair, Robyn Gold, Tricia Weise, Dave Skinner, Elaine Hagopian, Carol Coonrod, Mindy Clark, and Linda Clingan. Not pictured: Jim Turnbull and Debbie Neiger.

Ugliest Man on Campus

Each spring in support of the Summer Cal Aggie Camp for underprivileged children, each dorm on campus nominates a student for the "Ugliest Man on Campus" trophy. Then, the candidates must collect as much money as they can for two weeks. The dorm with the most money wins a new television for their dorm study room, and the ugliest man wins the trophy and a year's subscription to Playboy magazine. My dorm, Beckett Hall, selected me as their nominee. We did all kinds of things to collect money. We performed serenades outside girls' dorms, cleaned girls' rooms, took girls on dates, and sold kisses. We won the competition collecting several hundred dollars for a good cause.

Radio/ TV Internship

In 1971, I became an intern at KCRA News in Sacramento, CA. First, I monitored the Associated Press and United Press International for breaking news, sports, and weather stories to be condensed into 10-30 second announcements to be read by on-air reporters. Then, as I became more experienced, I was sent out to the field to record stories as they happened. Questions were structured as if the on-air reporter was asking the questions in person. Two of my memorable stories were interviewing a bomb technician who disarmed a device at the Greyhound Bus station and interviewing Miss America at a public event. After the conclusion of my questions, I asked her at the end of the interview, "What are you doing tonight?" She was tongue-tied.

Before graduating from Davis, I had hoped to either go into teaching or secure a reporter position with KCRA News. However, teachers were a dime a dozen, and the radio job went to the grandson of the station owner.

The Dating Game

After graduating from UC Davis in June 1972, I moved back home. In August, I was on the Dating Game as Bachelor #2. The single gorgeous blonde asking questions of each of the three bachelors chose me, and we were supposed to go on a dream date to Leavenworth, Washington's Apple Blossom Festival. Unfortunately, for reasons known, she did not go on the trip. So instead, I took someone I knew, and we had a wonderful time. A side note: I interviewed the same gorgeous blonde three years later for a crime report while working in North Hollywood Patrol.

Becoming a Police Officer

In November 1972, while working at a Department Store, I observed a man grab his chest and collapse. My Boy Scout training was handy, and I started CPR on the man. Just then, LAPD Officer Richard Root arrived on the scene and took over. After an ambulance crew took the victim away, Officer Root thanked me for my quick response and said I would make a good policeman. The officer gave me his business card and told me I was a good candidate for the Los Angeles Police Department. I applied, and on February 20, 1973, I began my career with the LAPD; graduating from the Police Academy on June 29, 1973; and transferred to Southwest Division Patrol.

After completing an 18-month probationary period as a policeman, I qualified to hold a side job known as "Moonlighting." Reporter Barbara Riegelhauft, with the Valley News, penned "Moonlighters See Two Faces of the Job Market, in acting, announcing, and a mortician." My first moonlighting job occurred after Los Angeles Valley College Football Coach John Becker asked me to be the stadium announcer for the Monarch's home football games. Valley had a star player named Jeff Fisher, who went on to coach in the NFL. In 1978, Mike Wyma of the Valley News did a story on me, dubbing me "Announcer-Cop."

Lou McClary

While announcing one of the Monarch's football games, John Ramsey's uncle walked his dog past the stadium and thought the announcer was John. Hoping to see his nephew, he went to the press box but was surprised to find me. He talked to me for about an hour while I announced the game. He was amazed at how similar my announcing and timing sounded to John. A few months later, he was at a family gathering and ran into his nephew, who told him about a policeman he met who sounded just like him. Unbeknownst to him, John was anxious to find a backup voice to announce upcoming games as his top backup moved to Hawaii. So, John reached out to the only LAPD officer he knew, Detective Sergeant Louis "Lou" McClary, who worked in Robbery-Homicide. Earlier that day, I chased and caught a robbery suspect and transported him to Robbery Homicide. After waiting to see detectives, I wrote up the robbery report for McClary. Lou read it and stated, "I won't forget you, kid (referring to me)." I then returned to North Hollywood Division. John then called McClary, who telephoned me and told me to be at Dodger Stadium for a tryout as John's backup public address announcer. For a moment,

I thought this was a great gag until I got a credential from the Los Angeles Dodgers in the mail.

I arrived at Dodger Stadium early and reported to the field. The Dodgers were playing the Cincinnati Reds. I noticed three other individuals standing next to John Ramsey. I walked over to John, and he handed me the lineup sheet and told me to go out to the home plate area and announce the starting lineups. In the fashion that John employed, I announced, "Ladies and Gentlemen, welcome to beautiful Dodger Stadium, home of your Los Angeles Dodgers. Get out your scorecards, and I'll give you the starting lineups for today's game."

After completing both lineups, I looked toward John and did not see the other would-be announcers. Fans in the stands were confused. They thought they heard John's voice, but his lips were not moving. John then showed me the procedure of announcing

Figure 4: At one of the Los Angeles Raiders games at the Coliseum, NFL Security Rep Lou McClary was my link to becoming John Ramsey's backup announcer which opened the door to announcing the Raiders and other teams.

the national anthem singer and how to depart the field to a waiting elevator to go up to the press box. Then, as the anthem singer completed the anthem, John would be in the press box to thank the singer and make game announcements. John then had me announce three innings of the game until he felt confident. I was dumbfounded when he asked me to substitute for him on Sunday for the Dodgers-Reds game while John announced the Los Angeles Rams game at the Coliseum.

Vin Scully

I arrived at Dodger Stadium early and ate breakfast in the press lounge. While nervously eating my scrambled eggs, the Dodger's famous radio play-by-play announcer approached me and asked if he could sit with me. He then said he had never seen me at Dodger Stadium before. I explained I was substituting for John Ramsey. We talked for 20 minutes, and he asked me about my job as a policeman, upbringing, and family. It seemed like my eggs were not entering my mouth because of my nervousness. He then stood up, put one of his hands on my shoulder, and said, "Son, you are going to have a great game." He then walked away. The gentleman was Vin Scully, the Dodger's radio broadcaster.

After his touch and words, it felt like all my butterflies were gone. Full of confidence, I went down to the field to welcome everyone, announce the starting lineups, and make pregame announcements without a hitch. Then, after announcing the national anthem singer, I left the field and headed up to the elevator. I asked the operator to take me to the press box. The operator said "no" as he was waiting for Mr. Ramsey. I told him I was substituting for John. He said he heard John's voice and would wait for him. I told him I must go up now, but instead, he directed me to a stairwell. Not wanting to be late to the press box, I hustled up the stairs, some three at a time. It was good I was still in shape from the police academy, or I would never have made it on time to thank the anthem singer. As I stood there with beads of sweat on my face trying to compose myself, Helen Dell, the Dodgers Organist, and Fred Claire, the Operations Director, looked at me and almost said in unison, "Do you always get this nervous when you announce?" When I told them I had to use the stairwell, they said, "We have a stairwell?" They then asked why I did not take the elevator. I told them the operator would not take me up. After that, the elevator operators and ushers were introduced to me so I would not be stranded again.

Well, the game went on. I did not tell anyone I was announcing the game, especially if I messed up. Around the third inning, I could hear the radio broadcasts by Vin Scully talking about me and describing my police work and growing up in the San Fernando Valley. The game went smoothly. Dodger personnel and the press congratulated me on my first game. When I got home, my answering machine had almost a hundred calls. Most of the calls were from fellow officers wanting tickets to Dodgers games. One caller was LAPD Chief of Police Edward M. Davis, who stated he was very proud of me and put the LAPD in a good light. He chuckled, then asked if I could get him tickets behind home plate.

Backing up John Ramsey

After that, John asked me to be his backup announcer for the Dodgers, California Angels, USC football and basketball, Lakers, Rams, Los Angeles Kings, Strings Tennis, and Los Angeles Aztecs soccer. In some games, John would have me announce the final period or quarter to give him a break or chance to beat the crowd out of the parking lot. John also had me fill in for him during intermissions of ice hockey or halftime entertainment at basketball games. For example, during one L.A. Kings season, I was the voice of a robot wherein fans would shoot pucks at a goalie dressed as a robot and try to score.

A real highlight of subbing for John was Bob Steiner, Jerry Buss' Executive Assistant, asking me to announce Game #6 of the National Basketball Association Championship between the Philadelphia 76ers and the Los Angeles Lakers. Lakers players included Magic Johnson, Jamaal Wilkes, Norm Nixon, Bob McAdoo, Kurt Rambis, Clay Johnson, and Kareem Abdul Jabbar. The 76ers included Julius Irving, Andrew Toney, Maurice Cheeks, Bobby Jones, Daryl Dawkins, and Clint Richardson. I then got to proclaim at the end of the game, "Your World Champion, Los Angeles Lakers!" Sportswriter Bob Trostle of the Burbank Daily Review did a story on me "Officer finds sports niche and Calls 'em as he sees 'em." I was John's backup voice for the next four years.

One of the highlights of announcing the Dodgers was the "Four Masters," Reggie Smith, Steve Garvey, Ron Cey, and Dusty Baker after they had set the Major League record of four hitters hitting more than 30 home runs in a season.

Freeway Series

On occasion, the Dodgers had me announce games whenever their regular stadium announcer was ill or had a conflict in his schedule. On April 3 and 4, 2012, I did the "Freeway Series" between the California Angels and the Dodgers. A familiar face, Vin Scully, saw me in the press box and asked what I was doing there. When I told him I was filling in for the series, he asked about my family by their names and how I was doing in police work. I was amazed at Vin's recalling abilities.

Pope John Paul II

Figure 5: From my vantage point the Pope was
driven around Dodger Stadium in the
"Popemobile."

On September 16, 1987, his Holiness, Pope John Paul II, helicoptered to Dodger Stadium to celebrate a mass for the people of Los Angeles. Security for the event was unprecedented. Of course, my being a police officer and an announcer was part of the security plan. I announced the Pope's entry and exit from the stadium.

Chapter 2

The Police Academy

Immediately after an oral interview by two officers and a citizen, I received a passing score of 93 out of 100. Next was a lengthy background examination wherein they interviewed family members, teachers, neighbors, and acquaintances. If you survived that, a polygraph and then an exam by a psychiatrist. A week later—no fanfare—an officer telephoned me to report to the police academy in a business suit.

Class 2-73

I entered the Los Angeles Police Academy on February 20, 1973, at 0430 hours (4:30 am). It was a tradition that the first of the five months of training begins at the earliest time of day. Our drill instructor, Officer Gary Perkins, was a former Marine Corps Drill Sergeant who kept us guessing every moment of our training. My classmates and I arrived in ties and suits for the first week. The second week we were issued and wore khaki-colored uniforms that had to be wrinkle-free and have pressed creases. You did not dare to be late, not have your hair cut short, and shoes spit shined. Failure to follow every rule meant push-ups or laps around the track. The first few days of training were also an orientation to all the aspects of becoming a police officer, including paperwork. Later, we received an identification badge, handcuffs, and a pistol. After that, we were fitted for our formal dress blue uniform, started attending classes, and got lots of physical training. We had inspections regularly, were taunted, and performed marching on the parade grounds. I was a college grad, and military drilling was difficult for me and a few others. We had three squads of military veterans and one squad of college graduates. Guess which party had the most trouble? Our squad also received "remedial marching" instruction after the day was over.

During training, I resided in a guest house behind my parent's home in Panorama City. In the first week of my second month, to show you how stressed I was about being on time, I did not read the clock correctly. I woke up, looked at the clock, and thought it read, "4:00 am." Thinking I would be late for the roll call at 4:30 am. The correct time on the clock read "12:20 am." Not realizing the proper time, I shaved, showered, grabbed my stuff, and headed through my parent's house to my car. I thought momentarily, "Why are my parents still up at this hour? They thought I was sleepwalking. As I drove closer to the freeway, I saw a gas station filled with cars and thought that was unusual for the hour. Then, the announcer on the radio said it was 12:45 am. Realizing my mistake, I turned around and went home. My parents were relieved I was not sleepwalking. I never had that problem with time, thankfully, again.

On the day we received our badges, we sat anxiously waiting to see them. As an instructor distributed the policeman badges (today, they are police officer badges), Robert "Bob" Rieboldt, who sat behind me, received a policewoman badge. When asked if there were any problems, Bob was tentative in raising his hand. We had five female officers going through the training with us. Finally, after a laugh, Bob got his real badge.

The second and third months of the academy were another grueling time for me, especially physical training and running long distances. I had never run a mile before. I was having trouble keeping up and began feeling sorry for myself and directed before Sergeant Frank Whitman, who supervised recruit training. Sergeant Whitman, a stern yet sensitive recruit supervisor, suggested I take the rest of the day off and evaluate whether I wanted to continue training or resign. It was Friday, so I had the weekend to think about what he had said. I told my father that I felt like quitting. My dad then told me these words: "Finish the academy. If, after you graduate and you still want to quit, then quit. It is important always to finish what you start." So, on Monday, I returned to the academy and decided to do whatever came my way. It was the best decision I had ever made.

Figure 6: A rookie ready to hit the streets of L.A.

During the second month of training at the academy, each trainee was loaned to a patrol division for four Friday night shifts to get acquainted with the job. My assignment was North Hollywood Division. My training officer turned out to be a disgruntled veteran who preferred not to get involved with anything that required much effort. So, my shift was eventless. The following Monday, my classmates were asked by the trainers about what they had experienced.

Trainees had been in pursuits, robbery calls, and domestic disputes. I had nothing to report. After three Friday nights of doing nothing and listening to action-packed nights by my classmates, each Monday morning, I was not looking forward to my last night in the field. It turned out I had the same partner, and nothing happened during our shift, that is, until the final minutes. On the way back to the station, a radio call was broadcast by a vice unit, requesting transportation for several arrestees at the "Hideaway Bar," a topless/bottomless strip club. Then, we got the call. My partner was not happy. He did not like transportation calls.

Upon arrival at the bar, a plainclothes vice officer walked up to our patrol car and told me to come with him. I followed him into the bar and to the back office and was stunned to see five naked women in handcuffs standing there. The officer then told me to remove each woman's handcuffs individually and monitor each woman as they dressed, ensuring they did not hide contraband or a weapon in body cavities or their clothing as they dressed. As I followed his instructions, a woman "cat-called" me and made my face even brighter red than it already was. The following Monday morning at the academy, instructors asked the class to tell their experiences as they had done in prior weeks. I did not say a word.

Unbeknownst to me, one of the instructors telephoned my partner and learned of the intimate details of my last call at the Hideaway Bar. One of my instructors, Bob Clark, then told me to tell the class what happened. When I finished, my classmates said they would have traded all their experiences to have been at my last call instead.

During the fourth month of the academy, recruits were loaned to a division to work patrol for three weeks and one week in a homicide unit. They sent me to one of the city's busiest divisions southwest, located in South Central Los Angeles. The fast pace of Southwest Patrol was challenging and fun, and I learned a lot. In the homicide unit, I will never forget one call, especially. In a death investigation, it is the responsibility of the police to evaluate the circumstances to see if the death was a homicide, accidental, or natural. Detectives took me to a death investigation and determined, with the advice of a Coroner Investigator that the decedent had died of natural causes. The decedent was a male adult in his thirties and over six feet five inches tall. He was in rigor mortis, wherein the joints of the body stiffen, lasting one to four days. The investigator had difficulty positioning the decedent on the gurney to remove him from the room. The only way to remove the decedent from the room was on his feet. The investigator teetered the decedent on his feet through the door to the gurney. The detectives assisted the coroner in moving the decedent's outstretched arms inward. Simultaneously, the decedent suddenly made a loud "moaning" sound as the air went from his lungs out his mouth. I was out the door in a flash. Family members in the living room wondered what was going on. Outside, the detectives roared with laughter as I huffed and puffed, trying to regain myself.

Southwest Division, earlier called University Division, was one of the busiest divisions in the City of Los Angeles. The demographics of South-Central Los Angeles consisted mainly of African Americans and a few Hispanics. The University of Southern California, its environs, and the Coliseum made up the north and eastern area of the division. Many of my training officers were African Americans. I had never worked alongside minorities, so I got on-the-job training I will never forget.

The Packer Family

Born in Burbank, I grew up in Panorama City, the eldest of two boys and a girl to Roy and Gladys Packer, members of the "Baby Boom" generation who had moved from Pennsylvania following World War II to Seattle and then to the San Fernando Valley. My choice to go into public service evolved from my parents' willingness to serve their country and my years in the Boy Scouts of America.

Figure 7: October 16, 1964, Troop 303 Court of Honor awarded the Eagle Scout Medal: kneeling from left: Alan Paine and Michael Zohns; standing: Phillip Walker and me.

My parents gave their all to me, my brother Christopher, and my sister Penny. We were all in the scouting movement, where I earned Eagle Scout, believed in God, traveled around our great country, attended the Boy Scout National Jamboree in Valley Forge, PA, and married spouses with the same values. My brother was in law enforcement as a Probation Officer and later as the Chief of the San Diego Office of the California Department of Insurance Investigations. My sister owned a prosperous flower shop with our mother.

Born in Pittsburgh, PA, in 1924, my mom, Gladys Geraldine (Allebach) Packer, served the home front during World War II as a registered nurse. While attending nursing school in Beaver Falls, PA, on May 31, 1943, she was in the delivery room for the birth of Joseph William "Broadway Joe" Namath, later to become an NFL Hall of Fame quarterback.

Born in Freedom, PA, in 1930, my dad, Roy F. Packer, the youngest of nine brothers and sisters, enlisted in the U.S. Army and received his basic training at Fort Eustis in Virginia. He then went to Fort Davis in South Carolina for Officers Candidate School, wherein he graduated as a Second Lieutenant in the Artillery. He went overseas to the European Theatre with the 318th Infantry Division in December 1944.

On January 21, 1945, 2nd Lt Packer was awarded the Bronze Star Medal for heroic achievement with the 80th Infantry Division. Major General H. L. McBride stated, "Packer led his platoon into the enemy-held town of Burscheid, Luxembourg, to contact friendly troops engaged there. Packer then skillfully maneuvered his platoon into the outskirts of the town to a point where intense enemy fire delayed the advance temporarily. Then, with utter disregard for his safety, Packer made his way through enemy fire to the portion of the town under friendly control. Returning to his platoon, he so capably directed the advance against the strong points he had observed that he lost no men from his platoon and killed ten and captured 44 of the enemy."

On February 5, 1945, Lt General George S. Patton, Headquarters, 3rd Army, awarded 1st Lt Packer the Silver Star Medal for Gallantry in Action for leading a reconnaissance patrol across the Sure River near Wallendorf, Germany into the Siegfried Line (thought to be the first allied action into Germany). After intense encounters with the enemy while collecting intelligence and after a fierce battle, they returned across the river under extreme enemy machine guns and were wounded. On March 13, 1945, Packer received the Purple Heart Medal. Soon after, he was promoted to captain and earned the Infantry Medal.

My brother and I did not really know about my dad's heroics until he passed away at 89. While growing up, we asked him about the war, but he never explained his experience. His generation, called "The Greatest Generation," or "G.I. Generation," kept to themselves about the war. Then, when I was 16, my dad received a wooden crate sent to him by his sister in Pennsylvania. The chest sat in her attic for over twenty years until she passed. He was puzzled as to what was in the crate. When my dad returned from the reconnaissance mission near Wallendorf, they captured a Nazi Major and Colonel along the way back. He made them strip down to their underwear and bagged each of their uniforms, guns, and personal items they carried. The patrol crossed the Sure River with the prisoners in custody. Bullets strafed them, and several of his squad members, including himself, were shot in the legs. Upon reaching their lines, the military police took control of the prisoners. In the confusion of receiving medical treatment, one of the prisoner's bags ended up with my dad's possessions. My dad was eventually transferred to the Queen Mary, serving as a hospital ship, and traveled across the Atlantic Ocean to an army hospital in Tennessee. The bag was never examined and forwarded to his family's home in Freedom. His sister cleaned and ironed the uniform and placed the items in a white crate for safekeeping. The gun had rusted, but the uniform was in excellent condition. After going through the chest, my dad decided to give the contents of the container to a museum.

Chapter 3

Southwest Division

Figure 8: Los Angeles Police Academy Class 2-73.

After graduating from the Los Angeles Police Academy on Friday, July 6, 1973, I reported to my first duty assignment as a rookie, on the day watch, to Southwest Division, formerly University Division, on Sunday morning.

Jumper 54th Street Overpass

During roll call, the sergeant gave out patrol assignments. 3-Adam-91 was my assignment to work in a black and white patrol unit with Bill Hallett. 3-A-91's area was a mixture of residences and businesses in South Central Los Angeles, from Slauson Avenue to the north, Western Avenue to the East, the Inglewood

City Limits to the south, and west to La Brea. Bill Hallett was a burly officer with five years of experience on patrol. After receiving crime stats and other information, I went to the kit room to check out a police car, receive two sets of keys, and a shotgun and shotgun rounds. While loading the patrol car, I was shocked to learn Bill told me to drive. A rookie only got to drive a police car once they had at least three years on patrol. Usually, rookies rode as a passenger and "kept the books," i.e., do the report writing and be observant. As I slipped the key into the ignition, Bill strapped himself into the passenger's side and issued me a warning: "DO NOT TOUCH THE RADIO UNLESS I SAY SO." Next, Bill directed me to drive him to a market on the northeast corner of Figueroa Avenue and Vernon Avenue. Bill then "cleared our unit" over the radio with Communications (making us available for radio calls). Upon arrival at the market, Bill asked me if I wanted anything and told me to stay in the car and not to touch the radio under any circumstances. Ten minutes later, he emerged from the store with a quart of orange juice and a block of cheese. While eating, the radio came to life and reported three loud beeps announcing a "hot shot" radio call. The "link" (a police dispatcher) stated, "All units and 3A91, a Jumper, 54th Street Overpass, handle the call, Code-3." My reaction was to pick up the microphone and roger the call but was stopped by Bill saying, "Don't touch the radio." My heart was racing. Code-3 calls meant to turn on the red lights and siren, something I had never experienced before during ride-a-longs in North Hollywood Division during my academy stint and only got to do during driver training.

As I started driving out of the parking lot, I knew I had to turn left on Figueroa and south to the call. Instead, Bill had me turn right and head north to Figueroa with the flow of traffic. I needed clarification. We needed to go in a different direction. Then, the link came over the radio, repeated the call, and asked our status. Bill picked up the microphone and calmly acknowledged receiving the call. I asked, "Should I turn around?" Bill told me to continue north and had me turn on the red lights and siren. As we approached Adams Boulevard, Bill directed me to turn right, head east to Broadway, then turn right, telling me I needed experience driving in these conditions. Approximately 10 minutes later, we arrived at the 54th Street overpass over the Harbor Freeway. To our surprise, we were the only police car to have responded.

We saw a woman in her 20s straddling the overpass north railing over the Harbor Freeway. As I started to get out of the car, Bill put a hand on my right arm and told me to stay in the car. "If she jumps, the CHP (California Highway Patrol) will have to handle the call." Bill then rolled down his window and yelled at the woman. To my astonishment, Bill told her to "Go ahead and jump!" Fearing my career was about to end during my first hour of duty, the woman interrupted my thoughts. She yelled, "What did you say?" Bill again repeated, "I told you to go ahead and jump." The woman became so enraged that she swung her left leg back over the rail to the sidewalk, stomped to the police car, and started screaming expletives at Bill. She then turned and walked away eastbound while turning and yelling more obscenities and disappeared out of sight. Bill then picked up the microphone and calmly stated, "No jumper," and told the dispatcher we were available for calls. We then headed to our patrol area as I wondered what was next, and Bill finished his cheese and orange juice.

Recognizing Faces

August 9, 1973, on day watch at 1230 hours (12:30 pm), Willie Wilson was my training officer and let me drive the black and white. While heading east on Slauson Avenue from Western

Avenue, we stopped a motorist for a traffic violation at Grammercy Place. My partner walked up to the passenger side of the motorist as I approached from the driver's side. As I stepped forward with my left foot, I heard a citizen yell, "Look out!" Then, a drunk driver going eastbound in the middle lane on Slauson clipped me on my left buttock, sending me flying. Everything around me seemed to move very slowly as I bounced off the violator's car onto the ground. Finally, I could hear Willie yell, "Oh no, I let the rookie drive." The drunk driver said he tried to swerve to avoid striking the officer but could not change lanes because of heavy traffic. I was dazed, and everything was spinning when I opened my eyes. The next thing I remembered was being placed on a belly board by paramedics and transported to Daniel Freeman Hospital. I was then x-rayed and found only a slight concussion and numerous lacerations. According to doctors, I was fortunate to walk away from what I experienced without a significant injury or death. While I was lying in the recovery room, two visitors came in to see me. I thought the men were investigating the traffic accident. Later, I learned it was my Commanding Officer Stephen Downing and Deputy Chief Louis Sporrer for the South Bureau. Later, they said they would send photos to me to help me to remember who they were.

The Twilight Zone

In September 1973, after three weeks of recuperating, I was eager to return to work on the day watch as I traveled east on the deserted Santa Monica Freeway. As I neared my exit at Arlington Avenue, I could not believe what I was seeing in front of me. A wrong-way driver was on my side of the freeway, coming directly at me. Earlier, the California Highway Patrol observed the driver going westbound cut through a hole in the center divider fence caused by a drunk driver putting him on the wrong side of the freeway. As I maneuvered to the left, the driver moved to his right. Just as we collided head-on, I turned the wheel slightly to hit him at an angle. Later, the CHP told me the maneuver saved my life. Both cars were totaled, and the other driver was intoxicated, uninjured, and arrested. God watched out for me again as I was not injured. A CHP officer then drove me to work.

I was still on probation (rookie cops serve 18 months, including the academy). My two new training officers were Randy Lloyd and Ross Dedrick. It was their job to evaluate me monthly as to my progress. Both men were exemplary professionals with years of experience and personalities to match, who motivated me immensely and made it fun to come to work. My field sergeants were Eduardo Hernandez and Jack Schmida. Sergeant Schmida taught me, "Talk your suspects to jail." This phrase made my contacts in the field a whole lot easier.

Randy, Ross, and I were all assigned to 3-Adam-91 with Bill Hallett. Our patrol area was south of Gage Avenue, west of Western Avenue, and east and north of the City of Inglewood. It was a mixture of single-family dwellings, apartment houses, and businesses. On September 9, Ross drove me to the front of a large apartment complex at 3236 W. 60th Street and stopped. I asked him why we were stopping there. He then shared with me an incident on September 9, 1968, involving a rookie on his first day on patrol who responded with a partner to a prowler call at this location. The rookie and his partner maneuvered to the apartment of the person who made the call. Unfortunately, as they approached the apartment, a psychotic man suddenly fired a shotgun from an open ground-floor window at the officers and struck the rookie in the face. Other officers responding to the shooting risked their lives and rescued the officer from the line of fire. However, an hour later, the rookie cop died in surgery at the hospital. Ross' description of this tragic event underscored the importance of the dangers of police work and keeping my wits about me at all times. Unbeknownst to me, a few days later, Ross' advice would serve me well.

While on patrol with Randy, we were northbound on South Rimpau Blvd north of W.64th Street when we heard three loud beeps on our radio preceding a "hot shot" radio call of a robbery that had just occurred at a liquor store just north of us by two men in a vehicle. My heart was thumping harder. A dispatcher would then announce more details regarding the call and assign a unit to handle it. So, we headed in that direction. Just then, the two men described by the dispatcher speeded by us in the opposite direction. Randy did a quick U-turn, and we saw the vehicle pull abruptly to the curb. The passenger then jumped out and took off, running south.

Randy yelled for me to go after him. I did as I was directed and chased the suspect. We went through backyards, over fences, patio roofs, down driveways, and across streets, and finally, I tackled him several blocks away. Fortunately, the robber was more out of breath than I was, making it easier for me to handcuff him. When I searched his chest, back, waistband, and legs for a possible weapon, I found a knife and pocketed it. I then looked around and realized I was on a quiet street with no one outside. And I had no idea where I was. In those days, we did not have hand-held radios hooked to our equipment belts or cell phones. I thought about marching my arrestee down the street until I found someone or a street sign. I thought the robber might get an opportunity to escape, and I did not want to start running again. Then, I heard a helicopter and watched its orbit around an area several blocks away. I hoped it would eventually fly over me.

I realized I had to do something about my arrestee before he got any ideas and handcuffed him to a tree while I tried to figure out what I would do. I then went to the nearest house and pounded on the door while keeping an eye on the robber. The woman inside would not answer the door and told me to go away because I was not an Inglewood police officer. I begged her to call the police. To no avail, I must have sat on the curb next to my arrestee for 20-30 minutes trying to devise a plan. Finally, when the helicopter orbited closer, I stood in the middle of the street and waved frantically. I thought I was in the twilight zone because I could not believe the crew members could not see me. Finally, Randy drove up and asked how I was doing and how happy he was to see me. He told me later he kept circling the area each time, widening his search, and that I had gone over a mile in the opposite direction than when I started, and that's why the helicopter and others were searching for a different area.

3-A-9 Code 1

"3-A-9, Code 1" was repeated several times over the LAPD radio to an unoccupied patrol car for over an hour. In the 1970s, we needed hand-held radios for each officer to carry. Calls for service were broadcast on the radio in a patrol car or retrieved using a police call box on a street corner. Whichever way, once you got a call for service, you would be away from your radio until the call was over. An hour earlier, my partner, George Hypolite, and I were working "PMs" from 1500 hours (3:00 pm) to 2345 hours (11:45 pm). We responded to a radio call dispatched as, "See the man; unknown trouble" at a house in the historic West Adams District. From 1880 to 1925, the West Adams District consisted of huge mansions, craftsman homes, and bungalows featuring amenities like "beveled-glass China cabinets, marble fireplaces, and mahogany floors." The houses sat at the north end of Southwest Division and, in 1973, stretched from Figueroa Street on the east to Crenshaw Boulevard on the west and north to the Santa Monica Freeway and south to Jefferson Boulevard. Three radio cars, operated by two uniformed officers, each in black and white patrol units, were designated as "3-A-1", "3-A-6", and "3-A-9" and were explicitly assigned to the West Adams District.

Our experience told us an "unknown trouble" call could mean anything from the discovery of a dead body to a citizen concerned about unusual activity in the area or nothing at all. My partner, George Hypolite, a former junior high school principal and black educator who grew tired of coddling children in the Los Angeles Unified School District, wanted to be more proactive and serve his community, so he became a cop. George did not like "unknown trouble" calls one bit. George was superstitious and liked to hang back behind me on these calls. We stopped our patrol vehicle just north of the location and started walking up a path to a stately multi-story mansion resembling the Bates Mansion in Psycho. At the top of the steps were a screen door and a massive door with a knocker. I tapped the frame with my baton to get the attention of whoever called. The door slowly opened, and an elderly gentleman answered the knocking. I asked what the trouble was, and he stated, "My mother and father were fighting." My partner and I stepped back when we learned the gentleman in front of us was 84 years of age, meaning his parents were centenarians. He ushered us into a semi-dark room full of antiques which turned out to be original furniture from the early 1900s. There, hunched over in a deep leather chair, was an older woman who turned out to be the caller's 101-year-old mother. In a gravelly but sweet voice, she told us she had had an argument with her husband five days earlier and had not seen him since and was worried about him. When I asked where he might have gone, she said he did not go anywhere because of his frail condition. He was over 102 years old and was somewhere in the house. She and her son were afraid to look for him. My partner, shaking like a leaf, grabbed my arm and said, "C'mon, let's get out of here now." I laughed to myself and coaxed George to help me search for him. We started with the bottom floor, which turned out to be the basement. I had never heard of houses in Los Angeles with basements, so I was interested in exploring one. My partner said he would wait upstairs, but I told him to go first. He did not move. He did follow behind me cautiously. Every inch of the place was the original. Closets had incandescent light bulbs shaped like a "frosty" ice cream cone that still worked by pulling a string. As we progressed up from the ground floor, we came across hidden passageways, nooks, and crannies reminiscent of the Haunted House at Disneyland. Finally—we were not keeping track of time—we entered the attic, and there he was, sitting in a chair with his legs outstretched, and his head tilted back with his mouth wide open. We expected to find the old guy had long passed on. As I leaned in to check for a pulse, he suddenly awoke, groaning, and blinked his eyes. I shuddered a bit while my partner bolted out of the room. I envisioned a frightened cartoon character blasting through a door, leaving an outline of himself like cartoons. I half expected to find my partner crumpled up on the ground four floors down, but George was shaking just outside the doorway. After telling the old gentleman why we were there, he told us, "Well, after over 80+ years of marriage, whenever my wife and I get into an argument, I come up here, so I don't have to listen to her." He showed us around his attic retreat containing a bathroom, a refrigerator stocked with beer, cheese, and milk, his easy chair, bed, and a radio. From here, he could relax in peace for up to several weeks. We then told him his wife and son had not seen him for five days, and they were worried. He told us to "Let them wait." That was good enough for us, so we headed downstairs and told the missus her husband was alive and well upstairs and said he would come down when he was ready. Upon leaving the house, we were puzzled to see our patrol sergeant pacing beside our police car. He told us the Communications Division had been Code 1-ing us (Code 1 was radio jargon for asking for the status of a patrol unit) for over an hour and wanted to know what we had been doing. George and I looked at each other, and I told the sergeant. "It's a long story." My partner told the sergeant he would not believe what we had just experienced and told me to get in the car, and we drove away without another word.

Choose Your Words Carefully

In the center of the Southwest Division is the sprawling campus of the University of Southern California. At the northern fringe of University Park are numerous fraternities and sororities. As a result, many officers from the Southwest Division made it a habit to patrol the area. Some patrol units made a point of patrolling the area even though they were way out of their area.

In 1975, I put my public speaking ability to good use performing "Lady Beware" training at sororities on W. 23rd Street next to the USC campus. Lady Beware trained college women to develop the necessary attitude, skills, and knowledge to help them prevent becoming victims of crimes. In addition, being single, I had the chance to see and meet beautiful coeds.

On one training session at a sorority, I opened my Lady Beware program by saying the wrong word to describe the opportunity for officers to teach ladies about preventing them from becoming victims of crime. Instead of saying, "Infiltrate your sorority," I incorrectly stated, "Penetrate your sorority." The ladies laughed and made nothing of it. A week later, my commanding officer called me into his office. He started by saying he had just received a letter of appreciation from the sorority, praising me for my outstanding Lady Beware presentation. He then read out loud the first sentence of the letter. "We would like to take this opportunity to thank Officer Packer for penetrating our sorority." The captain then looked me in the eye and questioned, "Penetrate?" I told him I thought they meant "Infiltrate." He glared at me and then told me to leave.

You Never Know

In 1974, during Thanksgiving weekend, my partner and I were on patrol in the northern part of the division when we observed a young coed driving at a high rate of speed south on empty Figueroa Avenue. We activated our red lights and siren, and the woman pulled to the curb. My partner approached the woman while I checked the vehicle from the passenger side. The woman was hostile at first until my partner calmed her down. Finally, she said she was a USC student and late getting to Los Angeles International Airport to fly home for the weekend. My partner then performed a routine inquiry through communications regarding any outstanding traffic warrants she might have. The RTO stated there were several totaling $300. The woman was arrested and transported to the Sybil Brand Institute (Women's Jail). As she was processed, she burst into tears and apologized to my partner. My partner looked at me and frowned. He then pulled out his wallet and paid the bail. We then left without her knowing my partner had done this.

Months later, my partner got a bank check for $300 plus interest from the young woman and a letter of apology. Several years later, I learned my partner married the woman, and they have three children.

3-A-99 "Good Morning"

You are regularly moved to different shifts when you are a probationary officer. Now on the graveyard shift, called morning watch, I was assigned to 3-A-99, which covered the south and east end of Southwest Division, with training officers Don Watson and Barry Solon. On my first shift, I worked with Don. I worked the radio as we left the station, saying, "3-A-99, we're clear (ready for radio calls); good morning." The RTO (Radio Telephone Operator) said, "3-A-99 Good morning, Officer Packer," in the sexiest voice I had ever heard. Throughout the shift, every word she said to our unit was sexier than the last. When we went to the station to do a report, the Watch Commander warned me about being professional over the radio. I fell in love with her voice but did not know what to do. At the time, I did not realize that the RTO, a gorgeous blonde named Lori Blackwell, my training officer, the Watch Commander, and others were setting me up. When we went back out on patrol, I was careful about every word I said on the radio. Still, the RTO kept up her act and said, "3-A-99, what's the matter?" Every time I worked 3-A-99; the RTO kept up her show.

One night, we delivered evidence to the downtown property room, and I saw it as my chance to sneak into the Communications Division dispatcher's office to see the RTO in person. Again, my partner told the RTO I was coming to check her out. As I peeked into the Southwest Bay, another RTO had switched places with the Southwest RTO. When she eyed me and spoke, she did not sound or look like the woman I had envisioned. Then, to make things worse, when I got back in the patrol car and headed back to the division, our RTO asked over the radio if I was okay. I did not say a word.

The next night I was assigned to Station Security. Probationary officers were assigned twice a month to monitor the parking lots, gas pumps, and exterior. On cold nights I was not too fond of this duty. You were required to check the areas, sit in a guard hut, or walk around the station. But, for the most part, the shift was uneventful and lonely. Then, an Italian catering truck pulled into the station's driveway at around 0400 hours (4:00 am). The driver got out and asked if I was Officer Packer. I said I was. He then opened the truck and handed me a box containing a lasagna dinner, salad, bread, and iced tea. I was dumbfounded. I told the driver I did not order anything. He said it was a gift from an RTO named Lori Blackwell and gave me a note. The note read, "Thanks for being a good sport." After that, Lori and I became lifelong friends and always laughed about her act.

Soup Bones

The next time I worked 3-A-99 was with Officer Barry Solon. As we readied our patrol car for the shift, I couldn't help noticing a large soup bone in a box on the rear passenger seat. I asked Barry what it was for, but he shook his head and said, "I'll show you later."

We cleared from the station, and Barry drove us to the south end of the division. We then turned right from Manchester Blvd onto Denver Avenue. As you looked up at the street, you could barely see anything. There were vacant lots, deserted homes, and trash everywhere. Police cars were equipped with a switch to turn off the brake lights. Barry flipped the switch and turned out the headlights but kept the engine running. I looked at him and wondered what was next. Then, several yards ahead of us were dogs. As we got closer, it was more like 30 dogs. The dogs looked confused. Then, suddenly, Barry gunned our vehicle speeding up to the next intersection. The dogs gave chase but stopped short of the corner, panting. Barry then droves us around the block to the point where we started. I was laughing uncontrollably. Barry gunned our vehicle again, and the dogs gave chase, stopping short of the corner again. Finally, after one more run and chase, Barry fed the dogs the soup bone.

I'm Watching You

One of my favorite partners to work with on patrol was a Black officer named Sid Oubre. We had long discussions about life, the people in the Southwest Division, and police work. The one thing he hounded me about was not thinking about dating Black women. Every time I sighted an attractive black civilian working at Southwest station, Sid would get on my case about it and say, "I'm watching you." Years later, he invited me to be the master of ceremony at his retirement dinner. Then, I met his wife, a gorgeous white blonde. He looked at me and said, "I gotcha."

The Alarm Clock

Working the Morning Watch from 11:30 pm to 8:15 am took a lot of adjustment as it changed the cycle of the circadian rhythm of sleeping and waking. At first, I had trouble sleeping during the day, which made me even more tired during my shift. In addition, testifying in court or activity during the day, like a doctor's appointment, caused me to sleep in the afternoon and evening.

To boost us during the shift, we were permitted to sleep during Code 7 (45 minutes for eating) in the Southwest Division parking lot behind the station at 4 am. The only drawback was that you had to sleep in your patrol car. So on one cold and rainy night, my partner and I were granted Code 7 at the station. We both fell asleep and fogged up the windows in our vehicle. When I awoke, it was daytime. I looked at my watch, and it was 3 pm. I then woke up my partner and realized we had slept over 11 hours. We then cleaned out our vehicle and crept into the station. After turning in our vehicle keys and shotgun, we tiptoed to the locker room and changed clothes. We were elated that no one saw us enter the station or leave to go home. That night we both worked the Morning Watch and sat at the back of the room with our heads hanging low during roll call. At the end of the roll call, Sergeant Jack Schmida held up an alarm clock. He then stated if you take Code 7 to sleep at the station, you may use this clock to ensure you wake up in time. He said, "I won't mention any names, but two of our Morning Watchers slept over 11 hours last night, and we don't want you to miss anything." Those in the roll call room roared with laughter.

The answer to my difficulty sleeping was self-hypnosis. An LAPD Captain was a master hypnotist, and after several sessions, he taught me how to relax and sleep whenever I needed sleep. The techniques I learned still help to this day.

Chapter 4

California Angels

From 1976 to 1990, I continued backing up John Ramsey at California Angels games and the Dodgers. After John's passing in January 1990, I announced the Angels until the start of the 1995 season.

The Front Office

During my years announcing at Anaheim Stadium, I was proud to have worked with five of the most excellent front office executive personnel Red Patterson, Marketing Executive; Tom Seeberg, VP of Civic Affairs; Tim Mead, VP of Communications; Lynn in Promotions; and Janet German, Secretary. Each of them handled my questions and made my job easier.

Law and Order in the Anaheim Press Box

Figure 9: Judge Phil Petty, John Ramsey, and me.

In an article in the Angels 1977 program entitled, "Petty to Ramsey to Packer – Angels Utilize Trio of PA Announcers." The story stated, "The Angels' trio of 'designated voices' has more in common than a pleasant speaking voice—they all are in the form of the travel business. Ramsey operates the Cerritos Travel Agency. Packer cruises the streets of North Hollywood in a black-and-white patrol car, and Petty can send you packing—he's a judge in the North Orange County Municipal Court. All three men treat the job as a hobby, although it is a bit more complicated for John because he announces several other professional and collegiate teams. The Los Angeles Herald Examiner proclaimed in their "Angels Notebook" on April 23, 1977, "There is law and order in the Anaheim press box."

Dave Strege, reporting for the Orange County Register, wrote an article titled, "Packer's as good as his words. PA announcer often is confused with Ramsey." "Don't feel bad if you've thought Ramsey was the man behind the microphone or if you sometimes marveled at how Ramsey could be in two places at once. People make the mistake all the time of John and Dennis sounding alike. As it turned out, Packer became the protege of a pro. Ramsey helped Packer along in the big time. I'd pick at him, says Ramsey. I'd tell him; you're doing this wrong or that wrong. Packer mostly does it right nowadays, with that familiar Ramsey flair." Another case of mistaken identity occurred at a Dodgers game when LAPD Chief of Police Daryl F. Gates was preparing to throw out the first pitch. Gates said to me, "I 've heard your voice everywhere in Los Angeles, and it's a great honor to meet you." Gates thought Dennis was John Ramsey. Packer replied, "You've already met me," and showed the Chief his badge. Gates then jokingly asked Packer if he had a work permit. Then Gates said, "Can you get me some good World Series tickets?"

Shay and Joe at the Angel Hammond Organ

Figure 10: Shay Torrent and Joe Tripoli.

Opposite my booth in the press box sits the organist. The Angels had two talented organists, Shay Torrent, and Joseph Anthony "Joe" Tripoli. Shay was the original organist for the Chicago White Sox (1960-1966) and California Angels. Shay resided in Santa Barbara, traveled to Anaheim, and stayed in an RV during a homestand. Joe lived in Burbank and composed music. I met Joe when he played the organ at the Forum in Inglewood for the Los Angeles Kings. Joe's final 7th-inning stretch at Anaheim Stadium, "Take me out to the ballgame," was in 1996. An intercom allowed us to communicate before and during games, so I would not talk over the organ and vice versa. While subbing for John Ramsey at an Angel game, Bobby Bonds Sr. heard me make an announcement and thought I was John. He walked into my booth and asked where John was. I told him John was not there. He stepped out of the booth, and I made another announcement. He returned and said he had just heard Ramsey make an announcement. I could not pass up the opportunity to kid Bobby, so I keyed the intercom while telling Bobby that Joe pulled a stop on his organ that plays John making an announcement. Bobby then stepped into Joe's booth. Joe said, here, I'll draw a stop on the organ so John can make an announcement. As he pulled to a stop, I made another announcement. Bobby was mystified and walked away. Later, the event John was announcing was over, and he walked into the press box and sat next to Bobby. Bobby asked John about the organist pulling a stop for John's announcements and thought that was clever. John looked at Bobby and thought he was nuts. John told Bobby about me subbing for him. Bobby realized then he had been fooled. He walked over to our booths, gave us both a mean look, smiled, and said he would get us back one day.

Highlights of 18 Seasons

September 25, 1979, the game I announced between the Kansas City Royals and California Angels was exceptional because the Angels clinched their first championship as the American League Champions. Frank Tanana pitched a five-hit, one-run game. In addition, Angels Don Baylor, Rod Carew, Larry Harlow, and Brian Downing had hits that moved baserunners and scored.

Figure 11: Pitcher Jerry Reuss started the season with the White Sox before being traded to the Brewers. Drafted by the Cardinals, he played for the Astros, Pirates, and Reds before becoming a Dodger and then an Angel. We became good friends.

In 1987, while doing the starting lineups during pregame, Angel pitcher Jerry Reuss stood in front of me, sucking on a lemon just as I was announcing, "At catcher, Number eight, Bob, Bob Bab-boone" (Bob Boone), came out of my "puckered" mouth. Later, he gave me an autographed picture of himself with the words, "Don't quit your day job. Your pal in fun & games."

September 29, 1987, Dave Shefter with the Glendale News-Press reported that the Angels and Valvoline Motor Oil sponsored a contest wherein the winner got to be the public address announcer at an Angels game with the Chicago White Sox. The contestant, a bank employee from Glendale, CA, won. When he arrived at Anaheim Stadium, I gave him some pointers for announcing. After announcing, he said, "The job isn't a piece of cake. You have to be watching the game the whole time. You have to be right on top of the player changes, following the batting order, and there's much more to do than you think."

It was fun announcing "Old-Timers" games that brought back the stars from my childhood memories. Duke Snider, Tommy Davis, Bill Rigney, Edie Matthews, Jay Johnstone, Joe Dimaggio, Dean Chance, Tony Oliva, Cookie Rojas, Al "Mad Hungarian" Hrabosky, Tito Francona, Milt Pappas, Luis Tiant, Joe Torre, Bob Gibson, Ralph Branca, Warren Spahn, and Bo Bilinsky to name a few. I even got an autograph from Mamie Van Doren, Bo's fiancée.

Another unique aspect of being the announcer is meeting notable people and celebrities. My announcing booth was next to Autry's private in the press box. Meeting Gene and Jackie Autry was extraordinary. When old western cowboy friends Buddy Ebsen, Denver Pyle, Glen Campbell, Pat Butram, Richard Farnsworth, and Iron Eyes Cody visited, Gene invited me into his booth. I once commented about seeing an old western where Gene ran down the street, hopped on the back of a horse, and rode out of town with no hesitation. Gene told me, "Today, I couldn't jump or hop on the back of a Chihuahua." On another occasion, former President Richard M. Nixon got the schedule wrong with the Autry's and joined me in my booth for a couple of innings. He autographed a baseball for me.

The 1980s saw Wally Joyner at First Base, Bobby Grich at 2nd Base, Dick Schofield at Shortstop, Doug DeCinces at 3rd Base, Brian Downing in Left Field, Fred Lynn in Centerfield, Devon White in Right Field, Reggie Jackson the Designated Hitter, Bob Boone at Catcher, Pitchers Chuck Finley, Kirk McCaskill, Mike Witt, Geoff Zahn, and Ken Forsch, Relief Pitchers Bryan Harvey and Donnie Moore, and Manager Gene Mauch.

I got to the ballpark early on a Sunday before the game. I conversed with Angels Manager Gene Mauch in the Angels dugout when Reggie Jackson came out of the tunnel and selected a bat for batting practice. Reggie then turned in my direction. He looked as if he was looking straight at me, and I greeted him. To my surprise, he said gruffly, "Who are YOU looking at?" I shrugged, and he said, "You don't talk to me unless I talk to you first. You ruined my concentration," and then walked to the batting cage. Gene turned to me and said it was not right how Reggie treated you. But you must get even. So, during pregame, I came up with an idea to get even. While introducing the Angels' starting lineup, I announced the players as I usually did by emphasizing each player's spot in the batting order, number, position, and name. When I got to Reggie, fans could barely hear me say, "Batting fourth, the designated hitter, #44, Reggie Jackson." The next batters, I emphasized loudly. During the game, I again announced players as they came to bat. One of the batters got on base, so it came time to re-introduce Reggie, which I read in a barely audible voice. After the third out, the telephone in my booth started ringing. I picked up the line, and it was Reggie. He said, "Dennis, I apologize for barking at you. You can talk to me anytime you want." After that, Reggie came to bat, and I emphasized him like I did the other players. I ran into Gene later, and he patted me on the shoulder and said, "Way to go!"

Milestones by players are another fun part of announcing. On June 18, 1986, Angel Pitcher Don Sutton became the 19th player in major league history to win 300 games by beating the Texas Rangers 5-1. In addition, I announced the retirements of Don Sutton, Bobby Grich, and Nolan Ryan.

Three days of exciting events led to the 60th All-Star Game at Anaheim Stadium on July 11, 1989. Sunday was an Old-Timers game featuring Warren Spahn, Johnny Mize, Gaylord Perry, Joe Dimaggio, Ernie Banks, and Joe Garagiola. Monday was an All-Star workout and home run hitting contest. Finally, Tuesday was the All-Star game. My brother Chris and his son Jimmy Packer were my guests and came by train from San Diego. President Ronald Reagan joined the Autry's. The All-Stars included Bo Jackson from the Kansas City Royals; Mark McGuire from the Oakland Athletics; Orel Hershiser, Joe Amalfitano, and Tommy Lasorda from the Dodgers; Mike Scott from the Astros; Rick Reuschel from the San Francisco Giants; Ryne Sandberg from the Chicago Cubs; Jack McKeon from the San Diego Padres; Vince Coleman from the St. Louis Cardinals; Von Hayes of the Philadelphia Phillies; Tim Burke from the Montreal Expos; and Kirby Puckett from the Minnesota Twins. The Disneyland Band and All-American College Band performed during pregame under the direction of Dr. Arthur C. Bartner. I announced the pregame, including introductions of the National and American League non-starters, managers, honorary captains, national and Canadian anthems, a jet flyover, the

Figure 12: Introducing Jay Thomas to announce a workout and home run hitting contest before the 1989 All-Star Game at Anaheim Stadium. My brother Chris and his son, Jimmy, were my guests.

umpires, first ball thrower, ceremonial first pitch, American League taking the field, and game's first pitch. The California Angels All-Stars were Devon White and Chuck Finley.

April 15, 1991 was the opening night of the California Angels' 1991 season against the Oakland Athletics. I was honored to meet and introduce Desert Storm Commander General Tom Kelly to throw out the first pitch during pregame.

Figure 13: TV personality Johnny Grant and Desert
Storm Commander General Tom Kelly with me in the
dugout.

Then, on May 1, 1991, I introduced the Treasurer of the United States to throw out the first pitch. She signed her autograph on a new $1 bill and gave it to me. Years later, she was indicted for money laundering.

On April 16, 1991, The Boston Globe made some observations about Anaheim Stadium. "They have lousy things going on at The Big A. They keep the restrooms clean, and the people serving beer wear ties. What is really appalling, however, is that their public address announcer tells fans not to use profanity or abusive language and to be considerate of their neighbors. What's happening to baseball?"

The "Voice of Authority" by Tom Singer in the September 1992 Orange Coast magazine sports article described every aspect of my role as a public address announcer and what I did in my day job—police work. PA announcers are like umpires and offensive linemen; anonymity means they are doing their job. "Take a hint. Next time you're in Anaheim Stadium and hear the public address announcement, "A polka dot Pacer, license number 2-M-R-B 0-0-7, is parked illegally and will be towed unless removed in five minutes, do what the announcer asks if the wheels sound familiar. That's Dennis Packer behind the threat. Detective Packer of the Los Angeles Police Department. Packers had to witness merciless beatings, tragic hit-and-runs, riffraff stealing, and hopeless desperation. And after the game, he had to hit the streets."

Because of my law enforcement background and position as the public address announcer for the Angels, I became a member of the Angels Speakers Bureau. It made it much easier to pass drug and alcohol-related questions to me to answer than for ballplayers to answer. For example, at a speaking engagement on April 9, 1992, at Sunset Elementary School in Fullerton, I was Master of Ceremony for a "Just Say No" drug prevention program with former First Lady Nancy Reagan.

Figure 14: I was part of the Angels Speaking Bureau
and assisted First Lady Nancy Reagan in drug
prevention programs at area schools.

On May 12, 1992, Janis Carr, a writer with The Orange County Register, wrote, "Policeman keeps order as Angels Announcer." "The voice. It's as familiar as peanuts and Cracker Jack to Angels fans. Nightly, during homestands, the deep voice booms across the box seats and reaches into the upper deck, telling fans who's up and what events are on deck at Anaheim Stadium. The voice belongs to Dennis Packer, a full-time Los Angeles police detective, part-time public address announcer, and big-time sports fan. For 12 seasons, Packer has been announcing the Angels lineup at Anaheim Stadium. In addition, he also works as the announcer for the Los Angeles Raiders and University of Southern California football games. He has served as the voice of the Los Angeles Kings hockey team at the Forum, the Rams at the Coliseum, and the Aztecs and Skyhawks soccer teams. He has also done the announcing at indoor soccer and tennis matches at the Forum." Her last question was, "Does it bother you to work in semi-anonymity that people know your voice but not your name or face?" I replied, "Not at all. John Ramsey taught me in the beginning that the public address announcer is the same as the scoreboard. You are there to help the fans enjoy the game and provide information. The stars are the players, not the PA guy. If you do something extraordinary, it upstages the game's real performers on the field, the court, or the ice. Just being here is exciting enough for me."

Figure 15: During the 1993 season a young blind fan named
Ryan spent the game with me in my booth.

One of the gratifying aspects of being the game announcer is meeting fans from all walks of life. I have encountered many individuals who desired to be a stadium public address announcer but needed the background. During the 1993 season, a young boy wrote a letter to the Angels wanting to meet me in person. His name is Ryan, a 10-year-old, and he is blind. His mother, Kate, accompanied him to my booth, and he sat with me for three innings. I was amazed at his baseball knowledge and what a game announcer does, and he seemed to know everything about me. Ryan displayed a great attitude toward life and was the happiest, making people laugh. A few days after his visit, he mailed me a thank you note written in braille and translated by his mother. On his 21st birthday, my wife and I attended a surprise birthday party for him. We continue to keep in touch.

Getting to the ballpark before games allowed me to meet and chat with players and coaches. In 1992, one coach, in particular, was Babe Ruth's roommate, Angels Conditioning Coach Jimmie Reese. Known as one of the most likable players in baseball, he spent most of his career in the Pacific Coast League, beginning as a batboy with the Los Angeles Angels from 1917 to 1923. Then, he played for six teams over his major league baseball career, including 2nd and 3rd base for the Yankees in 1930 and 1931, where he was the Babe's roommate. His batting average in 1930 was .346. Only Lou Gehrig and the Babe hit for higher averages on the team. He retired as a player in 1938. During World War II, Jimmie was also a veteran serving in the Army in 1942 and 1943. In 1972, at 71, Jimmie became the Angels' Conditioning Coach until his passing on July 13, 1994, at 93. Inducted into the Angels Hall of Fame, his jersey number, 50, was retired. Jimmie threw out the first pitch at the 1989 Major League Baseball All-Star Game, which I announced at Anaheim Stadium.

Figure 16: The California Angels Conditioning
Coach Jimmie Reese, who was Babe Ruth's
roommate when he played for the New York
Yankees from 1930-31.

One of my tasks was introducing and announcing the Upper Deck Heroes of Baseball and Oldtimer's Games.

July 21, 1993, while on vacation in Boston, Tim Mead arranged for my family and me to attend an Angels game with the Red Sox at Fenway Park. Before the game, I met the Red Sox's legendary public address announcer, Sherman "Sherm" Feller. A retired army officer, prolific songwriter, and host of a big-band-oriented radio program, Sherm announced the Red Sox from 1967 until he died in 1994. Sherm was known throughout the major leagues for his distinctive Boston-accented style of introducing players, saying their uniform number, full name, position, and last name when the batter stepped to the plate, such as "Number 8, Carl Yastrzemski. First base, Yastrzemski." You can hear Sherm's voice at Cooperstown's Baseball Hall of Fame.

I was thrilled when Sherm asked me to introduce the starting lineups and announce the second and third innings. Then, as I introduced the Angels' batting order, out of the corner of my eye (from 300 feet up to the press box), I could see the Angels empty the dugout and look up in my direction and point. Then, as I introduced the Boston lineup, the Red Sox wives sitting behind my wife in the stands told her that was the first time they could understand their husband's name. Later, the Red Sox communications director asked me when I would move to Boston. I declined.

Figure 17: July 21, 1993, while on vacation I met
legendary Boston Red Sox PA Announcer Sherm Feller at
Fenway Park. It was the thrill of a lifetime as Sherm had
me announce the first few innings of the Red Sox/Angels
game.

Other famous play-by-play sports announcers I met were William
Earnest "Ernie" Harwell of the Detroit Tigers, Harry Caray of the
Chicago Cubs, George Brett, Al Conin, and Don Drysdale of the
California Angels.

After announcing an Angels game at Anaheim Stadium, I drove to
the LAPD North Hollywood station to work the "morning watch"
shift (11:30 pm to 8:00 am). On my way to work, I listened to the
Dave Hull Show on the radio. Known as "The Hullabelooer" for his
funny antics, he recorded me announcing a fan warning before the
game. He played the recording and then asked the first person to
call in and guess the name of the stadium announcer would win

four tickets to the next Angel game. I was elated to hear my voice. After playing the recording, a fan called in and said the announcer was John Ramsey. Dave then congratulated the fan for guessing the correct answer. I was disappointed. Then, moments later, Angel's radio broadcaster and former Dodgers great Don Drysdale came on the radio and said to Dave, "You've made a terrible mistake. The announcer was Dennis Packer, who substitutes for John Ramsey. Watch out, Dennis carries a gun." Dave then said the caller would not receive the tickets.

After a couple of commercials, Dave pretended somebody was knocking on the studio doors and asked who it was. Then Dave said, "Dennis put down that gun!" Then Dave played several gunshots sound effects, then went to a commercial. Dave then cleared up the mistake and went back to his post-game show. A sergeant at LAPD's Foothill Division heard bits and pieces of The Hullabelooer's broadcast and called his friend at North Hollywood station. Sergeant Larry Phillips, the Watch Commander, was asked if he had heard that Packer had been in a shooting. Phillips did not and started the process of reporting a shooting. Phillips then began notifying his superiors of the call. About 30 minutes later, I arrived at North Hollywood station. As I entered the station, Phillips immediately had me go to his office and wait there. Another sergeant, Phil Butler, arrived at work and saw me in the watch commander's office. Sergeant Butler laughed and told me he had heard the broadcast and thought it was hilarious. He then told me to go and get dressed for my patrol shift. Butler then shared the story with Sergeant Phillips, who had to call his superiors and straighten out the potential mess.

Chapter 5

North Hollywood Division

Figure 18: Ready for patrol duty at North Hollywood Station 1975.

After 23 months in the Southwest Division, I was transferred to the North Hollywood Division in 1975, where I worked patrol, jail, and community relations until July 31, 1979. The friendships I made during my nearly two years at Southwest and four years at North Hollywood are still true today.

How to Handle a Woman Motorist

I never liked stopping women drivers. From Day 1, I learned three things that would get you in trouble: women, drinking, and gambling. Whether they had children in the car, were late for an appointment, were argumentative, or were sultry, I never liked stopping women. I guess it was my upbringing, respect for the opposite sex, or bad experiences other partners shared with me. And who could forget to stop a homemaker from running a stop sign with three kids in the backseat? Upon asking her for her license, she hiked her skirt up, exposing herself while asking for a break. It worked. I gave her a warning and got out of there.

My actual test awaited me on my first day in paradise. After 23 months in the Southwest Division, one of the hottest non-stop divisions, I transferred to what I thought were the quiet streets of North Hollywood Division. Here I was patrolling on day watch by myself as 15-L-49. The "L" signified a one-person unit. Throughout the morning, there were hardly any calls for service. Finally, I asked the RTO (Radio Telephone Operator) if my radio was working. She replied it was working fine and told me to call the Communications Division. So, I did, and they told me to stop bugging them and appreciate the quiet.

At about 1:25 pm, I left the station and headed west on Tiara Street. As I waited for traffic to clear and turned left on Lankershim Boulevard, a car driven by a woman whisked by me so fast in the direction I was turning she momentarily scared me. As I began to follow her and closed the gap between us, I estimated her speed at 60 mph in a 35-mph zone. Then, she abruptly stopped at a traffic light. I turned on my red lights and buzzed the siren to get her attention. When the light changed to green, she did not pull over and instead sped up again and continued southbound. At

Burbank Blvd, she barely made it through on the yellow light. As we neared the North Hollywood business district, now called the Arts District, I turned the siren switch to the public address system and yelled for her to pull over. I did not realize at the time every person inside and outside businesses along Lankershim heard my command and came out to see what the commotion was. At Weddington Street, she abruptly turned left and pulled to the curb in front of a bank. I pulled behind her and walked up to her open driver's window. Her stereo was up full blast. I asked her to turn off the radio and give me her driver's license, to which she replied, "I ain't givin' you no mother fuc (expletive) license!" Knowing most motorists would back down if a second officer was present, I went back to my police car on the passenger's side, picked up the radio microphone, and asked for a backup officer.

I forgot to turn the radio switch from the public address to the radio. So, I thought I was radioing for another unit but instead was talking to dead air. As I waited, I grew frustrated that there was no immediate response because if you asked for a backup in Southwest, you heard the roar of engines coming your way immediately. Then, in my peripheral vision, I noticed the woman get out of her car and approach me on the sidewalk. As I turned to face her, she was about five feet tall and looked in great physical shape. Then she got into a karate stance, and before I could do anything, she leaped up and karate-kicked me in the mouth, splitting my lip.

Unbeknownst to me, within seconds after her first kick, the manager of a liquor store across the street called 9-1-1 to report an officer under attack. In addition, a bank employee pulled the bank robbery alarm. Communications received these simultaneous calls and sent the cavalry to my location. Again, the woman got into a karate stance. This time, I was ready and caught her by the ankle and forced her to the ground. During the scuffle, an off-duty L.A. County Sheriff's Deputy ran to my open driver's door and radioed for help. The bank employee thought my police car was stolen and called 9-1-1.

I managed to get control of the female, get her handcuffed, and then place her in the backseat of my patrol car. After cinching up the seatbelt, I shut the passenger vehicle door. I dusted myself off and dabbed my lips. Then I noticed police everywhere. They drew their weapons in my direction, and a police helicopter hovered overhead. Thinking there was something else going on, I looked around and then saw a gray-haired sergeant, known affectionately as "Mother M," on the corner wanting to know, "What is going on here and who are you and what are you doing in North Hollywood Division?" He had never seen me before. I told him who I was and what had happened. He then radioed the helicopter and officers and calmed the situation down. As it turned out, the sergeant had more witnesses than he had ever encountered who stated I tried to do everything right, and the motorist was wrong. During the booking process at the station, I learned the woman was wanted on a felony warrant and had a lengthy criminal record, including assaulting police.

The following day at Roll Call, the assault on me continued. First, the watch commander announced to everyone in the room that I would be giving training on "How to Ticket a Female Motorist." Then, Richard Harris' vocal solo from the motion picture Camelot, "How to Handle a Woman," was played over the intercom. But the ragging did not stop there. For the next three weeks, every time a unit in North Hollywood stopped a female motorist, the officers would ask over the air for the RTO to send me to their location.

15-A-49 Where Are You?

In the early 1960s, the television sitcom "Car 54, Where Are You" aired on NBC. Fictional New York Police Officers Gunther Toody and Francis Muldoon worked the 53rd precinct in The Bronx and were forever lost.

In 1974, Greg Stahr and I were regular partners on morning watch, 2300 hours (11:00 pm) to 0745 hours (7:45 am), assigned to unit 15-A-49, which covered the central area of North Hollywood Division where streets run north and south and east and west. On occasion, the south-end units, covering the Hollywood Hills north of Mulholland Drive, would get busy, so we had to respond to calls they could not cover in their area. However, learning the streets in the hills took years because roads wound around curves, climbed hills, and could run in all directions. The best eating spots and unusual activity occurred in the south end, so we did not mind.

One night, just after 0100 hours (1:00 am), we received a radio call of a burglary in progress at a house up in the Hollywood Hills. Greg was driving, and I was the passenger officer and handled the radio communications. One of the problems with not working in the Hollywood Hills is knowing the streets; some are dead ends, and the direction of winding roads makes it difficult to see where you are going. As we neared the location and dimmed our lights, we could see three young men loading a van with televisions and stereo equipment. Then, one of them spotted us, and they jumped in the truck and took off. We gave chase, and I told Communications we were westbound; then southbound; then eastbound; but forgot to call out the streets. We felt like we were in a maze. When pursuits occurred in the San Fernando Valley, Communications notified units to switch to Tactical Frequency One (TACT-1) so as not to interrupt regular radio broadcasts.

When my partner called out the street name we were on, I gave it to the RTO (Radio Telephone Operator), and then we were on a new street and going in a different direction. Backup units responding to the Hollywood Hills kept asking for our location. Then we got on a winding lane, making it doubly difficult to know the direction and what roads we were approaching.

Finally, we were on Mulholland Drive, a narrow winding road atop the Hollywood Hills running north and south and could give a proper location. At Laurel Canyon Boulevard, the suspects turned south and headed toward Hollywood. At Selma Avenue in Hollywood, Laurel Canyon Boulevard turned into Crescent Heights Boulevard. Mind you, responding units from North Hollywood Division were on TACT-1, and police units from divisions south of Mulholland Drive, in those days, were on Tactical Frequency Tact-2. As we continued pursuing the suspects south, Hollywood, Wilshire, Rampart, and Southwest Division units streamed north on Crescent Heights and went right past us for nearly 20 miles. Finally, the suspects ran out of gas and surrendered in Gardena. Our only backup unit was from North Hollywood Division. Ten minutes later, police units from four downtown divisions and the California Highway Patrol surrounded us.

Do You Have Cats?

My partner and I received a radio call about a family dispute. Upon arrival, we separated the husband and wife to get each of their stories without interruption. While the wife was talking to me, I started to sniffle. I wiped my nose with a tissue, but the sniffling became worse. I then asked the woman if she owned a cat. She said she didn't. I then said there are two things I am allergic to, cats and marijuana. She blurted out, "The marijuana over in the top drawer of that chest (gesturing to the living room) is his." The husband then blurted out, "Yah, well, the heroin in the bottom drawer is hers!" The wife yelled, "The cocaine in the refrigerator is his!" He yelled, "The amphetamine pills in the kitchen cabinet are hers!" At that point, we handcuffed the husband and wife, recovered the illegal drugs, and transported them to jail. We booked the pair for possession of illicit drugs for sale.

In court, I was on the witness stand. One of the defense attorneys asked me, "Tell me, officer, do you expect the court to believe that you are like a K-9, able to sniff out drugs?" I replied to no. I was allergic to cats and marijuana. The judge said my reply was good enough for him, and the couple was later found guilty.

A Giant Black Spider

Like a box of chocolates, like radio calls, you never know what you'll get. "All units, a woman screaming for help and shots fired," was the dispatcher's information. Upon arriving at the call, a frightened housewife stood in the open-front doorway holding a smoking gun. We disarmed her and asked what was wrong. She said nothing and pointed into the house. My partner and I then searched the house, thinking we would find a person or persons shot to death. After looking in every room and closet, we did not see anyone. We asked her again what happened, and she muttered, "The bathroom." As we pulled the shower curtain away, we half expected to see someone shot full of holes. Instead, we saw holes in the tile. After the woman had calmed down, we asked her again what had happened. She said a giant black spider was on the wall and she tried to kill him.

A Misinterpretation

A photo appeared in the newspaper depicting me holding a suspect down on the ground, and the suspect was feeling extreme pain. If you did not read the caption and story below the photo, it looked like it was a case of police brutality. The watch commander got calls from citizens who were irate at seeing the picture of alleged excessive force.

Here was the back story: A robbery had just occurred at a convenience store, and the two barefoot suspects sped away together on a motorcycle. They skidded and narrowly missed broadsiding a car. At the same time, they both put their feet down on the pavement to stop but crashed. We arrived at the same time as the rescue ambulance. The hot asphalt had burned the bottom of both suspects' feet as they slid across the intersection. The paramedics asked us to stabilize both men by holding their shoulders while they poured peroxide on their feet to cleanse the wounds.

31 Single Women

Radio calls can take from a few minutes up to an hour. For example, on April 11, 1977, another radio call took two hours to see the victim of a burglary. The victim, a survivor of Auschwitz Concentration Camp in World War II, had his house broken into and several items from his incarceration stolen. After fingerprinting a glass case where the burglar entered, I contacted the watch commander to get permission to work on the matter further. My partner and I then drove around the area, gradually widening our search. Finally, about four blocks away, we encountered a male heroin addict carrying a bag containing the stolen items from our victim. The victim was elated with the finding. He offered to pay us a reward, but we could not accept anything.

A couple of months later, the victim called me and said he had just completed a 32-unit apartment building across the street from Los Angeles Valley College. He then asked if I would be interested in managing the apartments. I thought the rent I saved by being the manager might help me to save enough to buy a house. I answered yes to his question.

Another police officer I worked with, who had just divorced, shared the managing duties with me. He worked days and would cover the evenings, and since I worked the graveyard shift handled daytime duties. We shared a two-bedroom apartment overlooking the pool. We then set out to rent the apartments to as many single women as possible. I remember one of the women drove up in a sporty Porsche. She wore a miniskirt and was gorgeous. Being a manager was a good idea. We had the first cable television in the building and soon had ladies over to watch movies and bar-b-que steaks. Then, we found out why it was a bad idea to rent to as many women as possible.

The women started knocking on our door all day and night with problems, such as spiders, creepy sounds, ex-boyfriends, ex-girlfriends, divorcees, loneliness, and other complaints. It was like being married to many women at the same time. Finally, we got to the point where we found ourselves sneaking into our apartment, hoping no one saw us. My police officer buddy soon quit. Fortunately, a schoolteacher friend of mine, Ron Melin, needed a place and joined me. There were a few bright spots, though. One fall weekend, I had a nasty cold and was off work for a few days. The woman with the Porsche felt terrible and cooked me a home-cooked meal of crockpot chicken and soup. No one had ever done this for me before. Next, she asked me to open her door to accept home goods and furniture deliveries. I could not believe how clean and orderly her apartment was.

Respecting her privacy, I could not help but notice all the men who had visited her. Finally, I got the courage to ask her to come with me to pick out a Christmas tree for a needy family I knew. She and I had a great time and started to get to know each other better. Soon, we were dating, and then the unthinkable happened. She— Judy—and I bought a two-bedroom house together in North Hollywood. She moved in while I continued to manage the apartment house. I moved some of my clothes into the second bedroom. Her ultra-conservative mother stopped to see the house and growled at Judy about my clothes in a closet.

I regularly stopped by the house around dinner time and would stay until I left for work on the morning watch. We lived 10 minutes away from the station. One night, shortly after I left for work, a "hot prowl" burglar (a person who burglarizes homes with people inside) stood outside the front of our home. A neighbor watched him go to the rear and enter the house through an open window. First, the burglar went to the second bedroom and was preoccupied with a locked metal file box marked "Valuables." He did not know the box only contained greeting cards. When he broke the box open, Judy, sleeping in the main bedroom, heard the scuffling and thought it was me and that I had forgotten something. The burglar then entered the main bedroom. Judy had taken off her glasses and had trouble recognizing who it was. She then said, "Den?" When the burglar did not answer, Judy reached for one of my old batons propped against the bed and pointed it at him. He probably thought it was a rifle and ran to the window and exited the house. Judy then called the police.

We had just left roll call, and my partner, Willie Morstad, was gassing up our patrol car when a call came out over the radio, "Any unit in the vicinity of 121... Califa Street, a woman screaming for help!" Realizing it was my address, I jumped in the car, and we sped to my house, less than two miles away. My partner would tell me later that it was the fastest he had ever traveled in a police car. Upon arrival, there were eight police cars at my house. Judy's knees were wobbling when I got to her. She was okay. My sergeant told me I did not have to work the shift and to stay home with her. Judy's mother called the next day and demanded I move into the house. Six months later, Judy and I married.

The danger of living in your working division is that all the patrol units in North Hollywood made it a point to drop by at dinner time for a bite to eat. In addition, they woke us up at 6 am on weekends by making animal sounds.

Who is Making That Noise?

One of the most challenging aspects of working the graveyard shift was attending court proceedings during the day. The biggest problem was exhaustion from not getting enough sleep. Most of the court cases I was subpoenaed for occurred at the Van Nuys courthouse. Officers checked in before court began at 0830 hours (8:30 am). After that, officers could either sleep in cot rooms at Van Nuys Police Station or wait inside the court to learn where cases were assigned. For example, my partner Tom White, and I arrested a drunk driver set for a hearing before the court for disposition on Monday at 0830. At 1630 hours (4:30 pm), we were excused but ordered by the court to come back the next day. We did this on Tuesday and Wednesday, and now it was Thursday morning.

We were both weary. While we waited in the courtroom, we sat in the witness area behind a chalkboard on rollers. Hours passed, and we both fell asleep and started snoring. The judge demanded that the bailiff find out where that noise was. The bailiff rolled the chalkboard away, exposing two cops snoring. The judge then woke us up and sent us to her chambers. We thought we were in big trouble. She then asked us why we were sleeping in her courtroom. We explained we worked at night and were in court all week waiting to find out if the court would try our case. The judge then directed us to remove two blankets from her closet and nap on her two couches, and she would wake us at 4:00 pm. After that, she held the arrestee to answer and excused us for the rest of the day.

The next day, my partner and I arranged to have flowers and chocolates sent to the judge.

Recipe for Robbery

Willie Morstad and I arrested two male juveniles for conspiracy to commit robbery. We recovered from one of the juvenile's pockets a handwritten note titled, "ROBBERY EQUIPMENT." The note then listed the following:

- 2 PAIRS OF GLOVES

- 2 PAIRS OF SWEATPANTS

- 2 PAIRS OF TENNIS SHOES

- 2 SKI MASKS

- 2 PAIRS OF WHITE SOCKS

- 1 HANDGUN

- 1 SWITCHBLADE

- 1 BROWN PAPER BAG

- 2 MINNESOTA PLATES

- 1 ROLL OF SCOTCH TAPE

- 1 PAIR OF WIRE CUTTERS

The note included: "GET UP AT 7:30, DRIVE TO VENTURA AND WOODMAN (PARK), DRIVE AGAIN. PARK, GO IN, AND ROBB THE $$$. PUT IN FREEZER, LOCK BACK DOOR, RUN TO CAR, GET IN AND DRIVE HOME, THEN GO TO BED. THEN BE RICH FOR WEEKS TO COME."

Group Study Exchange to England

In 1975, I became acquainted with a neighbor in my apartment house, Jacques Abels. Jacques was a Studio City Rotary Club member and invited me to one of their monthly luncheons. I met the club president, actor Stacy Keach Sr., who asked me to speak on several occasions about policing in North Hollywood Division. We became great friends.

In 1976, the Studio City club, which was a part of Rotary International District 526, selected me to travel to England in a Group Study Exchange with four other nominees from other clubs in the district. An FBI Special Agent and I were the only law enforcement officers on the trip. LAPD Chief of Police Edward M. Davis wrote a letter of introduction for me. I served at Scotland Yard, was a bobby in Cambridge, the warden at Bedford Prison, a traffic officer in Oxford, and was an instructor at the Ryton on Dunsmore Training Academy. I stayed at the homes of law enforcement officials in seven cities in East Anglia and London.

Figure 19: LAPD Chief of Police Edward M. Davis congratulated me on my selection to the Rotary 526 Group Study Exchange to England in 1975—Jacques Abels on the left and Stacy Keach Sr.

On one of the side trips, the police wanted to thrill the FBI agent and me by having us go down an elevator shaft 998 feet to see what coal miners go through in a day's work. During the safety orientation, we learned that a canister attached to each miner's belt had a 45-minute supply of air to breathe in an emergency. But of course, I did not ask what happened after 45 minutes. Upon reaching the bottom of the shaft, we then crawled through a "facing." A facing is a hole two feet in height, several feet wide, and approximately 100 feet long, stretching to another mine shaft. A conveyor is along one side. Miners chip away with tools at the coal, making the hole bigger to get larger machines in to mine the coal. I was the first person to crawl inside the face. As we crawled, someone thought it would be fun to set off a charge of dynamite nearby. After setting off the dynamite, somehow, the FBI agent got ahead of me. I was elated to see sunlight after leaving the mine. I got a genuine appreciation for the job coal miners to do.

Figure 20: I have a new respect for miners after coming 998 feet up to the surface.

Upon my return home was the exchange of a uniformed "Bobby" lieutenant from London to Los Angeles. In addition, I facilitated the lieutenant's visits to numerous LAPD divisions. He got his thrill by being an observer in a police helicopter.

After the trip, I learned there were two finalists for the exchange to England. The other finalist was my captain of the North Hollywood Division. When I returned to work patrol, I found out the captain loaned me to jail for the next two months.

Youth Services Officer

In 1978, I was loaned from patrol to the North Hollywood Division Community Affairs Office as a Youth Services Officer. It was my job to serve as one of the advisors of the Law Enforcement Explorers Post and PALS (Police Activity League Supporters). Police Explorers is a hands-on program open to young men and women ages 14-18, allowing them to explore a career in law enforcement. Two explorers I worked with went on to jobs in the

US Air Force. In the PAL program, boys, and girls, ages 8-13 participated in several fun activities. We started a PAL Bicycle Drill Team reminiscent of the LAPD Motorcycle Drill Team. The "sting ray" style bikes were black and white. Maureen created a banner that led the bike drill team in the Hollywood Santa Claus Parade. Three of the PALS I really enjoyed working closely with were siblings Harry, David, and Betty Jo.

During my time as an advisor to the explorers, an allegation surfaced that a police officer was having an improper relationship with one of the female explorers. A witness stated the female was the passenger in the officer's brown Ford Mustang with a light brown top. I drove a copper-colored Ford Mustang with a beige top. Even though I vehemently denied the allegation, I was immediately reassigned to work at the jail as the investigation played out.

Unbeknownst to me, I felt like somebody was following me when I drove to and from work or was at my apartment. Later, I learned the Internal Affairs Division had surveillance on me, and they felt like they were following the wrong leads. While monitoring the female, IAD saw her enter a Ford Mustang driven by a tall, dark-haired male with a mustache that resembled mine. After stopping the car, it was not me but a patrolman working North Hollywood Division. Although I was vindicated, I went back to patrol with only an apology.

Ice and Grape Juice

July 31, 1979 was almost my last day on Earth. It was my last day on patrol in the North Hollywood Division. The next day, I would transfer to the Los Angeles Police Academy and promote from Police Officer II to Police Officer III. But first, I had to work patrol today by myself. I was the "U-Boat" on the day watch. The U-Boat is patrol slang for a patrol officer taking reports and doing fingerprinting at crime scenes.

After leaving the station, I headed south when a radio call came out, "All units, a robbery in progress at a supermarket at Lankershim Blvd and Magnolia." I responded to the command post and stood by until needed. The officers assigned the call quickly set up a perimeter and learned the suspects were still in the market. The officers then searched the market and asked for additional officers to assist them. I went with three other officers and searched the attic. It was over 100 degrees outside. Inside the attic, it was even hotter. After 20 minutes, two suspects were found and arrested. I was sweating like crazy. Then, I was assigned a call to go to the intersection of Coldwater Canyon and Sherman Way and direct traffic. After nearly an hour in the hot sun, I was relieved by a traffic officer and cleared to handle a report call.

Enroute to the investigation, I suddenly felt dizzy, and my heart was pounding. I then stopped at a fire station and told a fireman my symptoms. He had me sit down on the bumper of a fire truck and then told his captain about me as I started to faint. The next thing I knew, I was strapped onto a gurney, had an IV in my arm, and was rushed by ambulance to Riverside Hospital. Upon arrival, doctors and nurses began to treat me as if I had had a heart attack. Just then, Nurse Annie Owens interrupted the doctors and said to put me on ice as she recognized I was experiencing heat prostration. I was then covered with ice and made to drink pure grape juice. After 30 minutes, I was getting back to normal. Later, my sergeant drove me home. An hour later, Judy came home and asked me, "How was your last day on patrol?"

Chapter 6

The Fabulous Forum

From 1976-1978, I subbed for John Ramsey, announcing the Lakers and Kings at The Fabulous Forum in Inglewood, California. Then, in 1979, John was let go by The Forum, which positioned me to step in and announce, for the Kings full-time. I told John that they offered me the position and he said, "Go for it." It subsequently opened up opportunities to announce for the Lakers, Strings Team Tennis, Lazers indoor soccer, tennis tournaments, and the Davis Cup.

Behind the Scenes

Announcing also positioned me to meet many people behind the scenes. One was Lakers radio play-by-play commentator Chick Hearn. Known for "Chickisms" like, "You can put this one in the refrigerator. The door's closed, the lights are out, the eggs are cooling, the butter's getting hard, and the Jell-O is jiggling." Chick was always friendly to me and offered advice if I asked. Kings' broadcasters Bob Miller and Nick Nickson were also close and provided help whenever I asked them. I also got to know Head Usher Ron Mahkorn family and his son Robin, who operated the scoreboard. Robin later assisted me with USC and Raiders football as a spotter. Finally, Bob Steiner, Jerry Buss' executive assistant, asked me to announce Game #6 of the National Basketball Association Championship between the Philadelphia 76ers and the Lakers.

In 1979, Owner Dr. Jerry Buss asked me to help a new voice transition to announce the Lakers. Dr. Buss then doubled my salary with the Kings from $40 to $80 per game, which, at the time, was the highest compensation for a game announcer in the NHL.

You Sound Like God

Figure 21: Members of the 1978 Los Angeles Strings TeamTennis team with General Manager Jeanie Buss on the right.

I also enjoyed working for other Buss family members, especially Jeanie. She had me announce Strings Team Tennis, World Team Tennis, Virginia Slims tournaments, Michelin Tennis Challenge Series, and the Davis Cup as well as several tennis greats including Chris Evert Lloyd, Martina Navratilova, Billie Jean King, Bobby Riggs, Ivan Lendl, Jimmy Connors, and John McEnroe. During a tournament sponsored by Foster's Lager, I attended a reception before the matches and mistakenly drank one of the large Foster's cans and felt the effects of the beer. After introducing Martina, she commented that she had never heard her name pronounced so well. During a tennis match featuring on-court confrontational John McEnroe, he spent an excessive amount of time preparing to serve to start a game. Finally, the chair umpire signaled me to move things along, so I said, "Mr. McEnroe, it is your serve." John responded, "You sound like God," and started the match without further ado.

Now Skating on the Ice -YOUR Los Angeles Kings

Figure 22: "Now skating on the ice, YOUR Los Angeles Kings"
was my announcement from my position at center ice at the
Fabulous Forum. To my left, Penalty Timekeeper Lou McClary.

1979 was my first full-time season announcing Kings ice hockey at The Fabulous Forum in Inglewood. I loved being on center ice because the only thing separating me from the players was the plexiglass around the arena. A small hole in the glass enabled me to hear the referee tell me who scored a goal or committed a penalty. In addition, the atmosphere around me made the games more exciting; as it included the penalty timekeeper Lou McClary; penalty box assistants Ernie Rucks and Fred Hildebrand; scoreboard operator Robin Mahkorn: timer Bill Meuris; the off-the-ice officials Johnny Johnson and Denis Roy; as well as goal judges Rick Lundgren and Ed Lee. The cold from the ice surface and the action on the ice added to the thrill of the games. Lou McClary was also the security representative for the Kings in the National Hockey League.

Before the start of the Kings games, I considered it an honor to introduce opera singer Frank Mahoney to sing the Canadian National Anthem and the U.S. National Anthem. Frank's renditions were second to none. Forum organists Shay Torrent and Joe Tripoli accompanied him. My good friends Shay and Joe were also the organists at Anaheim Stadium for the California Angels.

Pronouncing Names

An essential aspect of announcing games was learning to pronounce the players' names correctly. Players from the United States and Canada were usually easy to pronounce. However, players from Russia and the former Soviet-bloc nations, Czechoslovakia, and other European countries could be challenging. And then, a player would come along with what looked like a manageable name to pronounce. For example, one season, the Kings acquired a defenseman named Randy Manery, a Canadian player. Usually, I would check the pronunciation of a name with coaches, play-by-play radio and television announcers, and a team's sports information director. This time, a 13-year-old hockey fan named Nick Rose approached me and suggested that I pronounce the player's name "Má-nary," whereas others said it was "Man-éry." So, while reading the starting lineups for the game, I pronounced his name as the teenager had pronounced his name. The player skated over to me and said I was the first announcer to pronounce his name correctly. From then on, I sought Nick's help in pronouncing player's names. Nick's family and my family became close friends over the years. Today, Nick is one of the top hand surgeons in the world.

Kings Highlights

There were many highlights during my 11 years announcing the Kings. Getting to know players personally was remarkably interesting. The Kings' "Triple Crown Line" of Marcel Dionne, Charlie Simmer, and Dave Taylor was exciting to watch and even more fun to know off ice.

Other Kings players were centers and wingers Bernie Nicholls, Luc Robitaille, Mike Murphy, Doug Smith, Jimmy Carson, and Phil Sykes; defensemen Dave "Tiger" Williams, Dean Kennedy, Jay Wells, Jerry "King Kong" Korab, Mark Hardy, and Rick Chartraw; and goaltenders Rogie Vachon, Rollie Melanson, and Mario Lessard.

Figure 23: NHL Hall of Fame Kings left winger Luc Robitaille in 1986 during his rookie season, was shot by Jayne Kamin Oncea.

Memorable hockey greats from other teams were Bobby Orr of the Boston Bruins, Gordie Howe and Denis Savard of the Chicago Blackhawks, Wayne Gretzky of the Edmonton Oilers, and Guy Lafleur of the Montreal Canadiens.

33rd NHL All-Star Game

February 9, 1981 was the 16th Lester Patrick Trophy Presentation and dinner. The following night I announced the 33rd NHL All-Star Game. One of the celebrities I introduced was Charles Schultz, creator of Peanuts and Snoopy, who drew me a personalized cartoon. The Campbell Conference, led by Denis Potvin of the New York Islanders and Bill Barber and Paul Holmgren of the Philadelphia Flyers, defeated the Wales Conference 4-1, led by the Triple Crown Line, Peter Stastny of the Quebec Nordiques, and Randy Carlyle of the Pittsburgh Penguins. Mike Liut of the St. Louis Blues was the MVP.

Sore Vocal Cords

There are consequences assessed against players for rule violations called "minor," "major," "10-minute misconduct," and "game misconduct" penalties. Minor penalties call for a player to go to the penalty box, giving the opposing team a one-player advantage. Minor violations include tripping, hooking, interference, charging, roughing, fighting, slashing, and delay of game. A player can receive a 5-minute "major" or a 10-minute misconduct. Also, a player receiving a "game misconduct" must leave the game. The referee tells the announcer the player's name and number, and indicates the penalty and length assessed. The announcer then announces to the crowd the team, the player's number and name, the duration of the penalty, and the time the penalty occurred during the period. The practice of announcing the penalty twice started in Canada, where it was told in English and French.

On April 9, 1981, during the first game of the Stanley Cup Playoffs at The Forum, the Kings and New York Rangers set seven penalty records. They penalties included:

- 19 most penalties in one period

- 43 penalties by two teams in one period (NHL Record)

- 59 penalties by two teams in one game (NHL Record)

- 104 minutes for most penalties in one period

- 125 minutes for most penalties in one game

- 229 minutes of penalties by two teams in one period

- 267 minutes of penalties by two teams in one game (NHL Record)

Figure 24: April 9, 1981, the first round of the Stanley Cup between the Kings and New York Rangers. When fist to cuffs start the players drop their gloves and sticks in this photograph by LA Times photo by Jayne Kamin Oncea.

Gloves, sticks, and helmets littered the ice each time penalties occurred. My voice was nearly gone by the end of the game.

The Miracle on Manchester

On April 10, 1982, the Kings pulled off a historic comeback in the Stanley Cup Playoffs, called "The Miracle on Manchester" (The Forum is situated on Manchester Boulevard), as they rallied from five goals down in the third period to defeat the Edmonton Oilers 6-5 in overtime in Game 3 of the Smythe Division Semifinals. It was exciting to finally announce the Kings' comeback. The Oilers scored five unanswered goals after two periods by Mark Messier, Lee Fogolin, Risto Siltanen, and Wayne Gretzky, who scored two goals. Assists were from Glenn Anderson, Kevin Lowe, and Randy Gregg.

Defenseman Jay Wells led the scoring for the Kings with the first goal at 2:46 with assists from Marcel Dionne and Larry Murphy in the 20-minute third period to make it 5-1. Doug Smith scored with assists from Mark Hardy and Jerry Korab, making it 5-2 at 5:58. Charlie Simmer scored with an assist from Dean Hopkins at 14:38 to make it 5-3. At 15:59, Mark Hardy, with assists from Steve Bozek and Larry Murphy, made it 5-4. With the Kings swarming and the crowd screaming, Steve Bozek tied the game with assists from Mark Hardy and Marcel Dionne with five seconds remaining in the third period. Then, at 2:35 in overtime, Daryl Evans scored the winning goal with an assist by Doug Smith. The Forum crowd went wild. The Kings went on to defeat the Oilers three games to two. The Kings were heavy underdogs to the Oilers in the series.

Smallest Crowd of the Season

On March 23, 1984, L.A. Times staff writer Sam McManis authored an article titled "Kings Perfect Against Jets-Winless" and "Smallest Crowd of Season Sees 3-3 Tie, Eats Free Hot Dogs." McManis reported, "Midway through the second period, with the Kings trailing 3-2, and the crowd being "lulled" to sleep by the boring play, public address announcer Dennis Packer announced that everyone in attendance would receive a free hot dog, courtesy of owner Jerry Buss. It got the biggest crowd reaction all night. Shortly after the announcement, many fans from all areas of The Forum left their seats and headed for the concession stands to get a free $1.25 hot dog." The Kings broadcaster Bob Miller commented that it looked like they just announced a fire in the building.

Jayne Kamin-Oncea

Another rewarding aspect of announcing games is meeting the people behind the scenes. One of those individuals, since 1980, was L.A. Times photographer Jayne Kamin Oncea. She and I met while I was announcing a police graduation that she was covering for the Times. Jayne heard my voice and thought I sounded like the L.A. Kings announcer. We have been close friends ever since.

Jayne's photography is second to none as she is able to capture the essence of a news story, family event, or sports moment in tremendous detail. Her photos of the Kings are exceptional. Her shots of LAPD recruit training were eye-opening. So, was I ever surprised on November 30, 1984, when Jayne shot a closeup photo of my 5½ month-old son, Brett, wearing a Kings cap at The Forum that appeared on Page 2 of the sports section, "Morning Briefing."

I was honored to perform Jayne's late husband Bill's gravesite eulogy. Bill served our nation honorably with the U.S. Army in Vietnam. Over the years, I also got to know Jayne and Bill's sons, Daniel, and Billy. Both young men have chosen law enforcement as their career with distinction.

You can view her exceptional work at fastjaynephotography.com.

JAYNE KAMIN / Los Angeles Times

Figure 25: November 30, 1982, LA Times photographer Jayne Kamin Oncea shot this closeup of my 5 ½-month-old son Brett in the "Morning Briefing" of the LA Times Sports Section.

"DA" or "NYET"?

During the start of the Kings' 1985-86 season, I learned they would play an exhibition game with the Union of Soviet Socialist Republic's Central Red Army Hockey Team on December 26, 1985. In preparing for the game, I thought it would be great to announce it in both English and Russian. So, to learn to speak Russian, I jotted down all announcements in English. I then gave the statements to USC Russian Professor Tanya Garbach, who translated them into Russian and wrote them phonetically. Allan Malamud, a sportswriter with the Los Angeles Herald Examiner, wrote in his "Notes on a Scorecard," "Dennis Packer will make his public address announcements in Russian and English at the December 26 Kings-Red Army hockey game at the Forum..."

During pregame warmups of both teams, the referee skated over to me and started talking to me in Russian. I had not prepared for this and responded to his statements by nodding my head and saying, "Da" (for yes) and "Nyet" (for no). I must have answered his words correctly because he smiled and skated away. The penalty timekeeper, timer, and scoreboard operator were convinced that I could speak Russian. I was getting nervous. Team introductions, penalties, and goals were each announced in Russian and English without a hitch. Then, during the third period, one of the Red Army players received a penalty and was directed to the penalty box. The player screamed at the referee and me his objections in Russian. Again, I responded by nodding and saying "Da" and "Nyet." Only this time, I must not have answered him incorrectly because he slammed his stick against the plexiglass. The referee then tacked on a "game misconduct" penalty, and the player left the ice, yelling and screaming. After the game ended, the head coach of the Red Army team, Victor

Tikhonov, walked across the ice to me and invited me to a reception with his team. Thinking the mad Russian would be at the reception, I decided it would be safer to skip the reception and go home. It turned out to be the right decision, as my daughter Natalie was born a couple of hours after I arrived home!

Los Angeles Lazers

From 1982-1983, brother Johnny Buss and longtime California Sports executive Ron Weinstein asked me to announce the Los Angeles Lazers indoor soccer team that played in the Major Indoor Soccer League.

Chapter 7

Training Division

After six years in the "field" (working patrol), I applied to promote from Police Officer II to Police Officer III as a training officer and staff writer at the Training Division. Staff writers are called "squints" because of an assignment to an office and having to squint when they go outside. A coat, tie, and a writing instrument replaced your uniform, gun, and baton.

Field Training Services Unit

August 1, 1979, was my first day as a staff writer assigned to the Training Division, Field Training Services Unit. The first year we were in an office inside the main building. After that, we were in the "Bat Cave" underground below the shooting range. The unit produced training bulletins and scripts for training videotapes. I was one of four police officers, John Lane, Jim Anderson, and Bob Rieboldt, who worked for Sergeants Bob Lowry, Rod Grahek, and David Bailey, and Lieutenants Ted Kozak and Russ Kindermann, who oversaw the FTSU. Later, Jim was promoted to patrol sergeant and was replaced by Stacy Morris.

My job was researching, writing, and producing roll call training videos about police work. My prior experience as a radio station intern really helped me in this new job. First, I created a script for a video between eight and ten minutes in length with an accompanying lesson plan distributed to training sergeants throughout the LAPD. The videos covered subjects like reenacting officer-involved shootings and tactics, new laws, equipment reviews, and courtesy. Once my sergeant approved a script, the TVPS (Television, Photo, and Sound Unit) would produce it. I was allowed to brief the TVPS crew director. Often, I would accompany the director in the field in creating each video.

In my first year at FTSU, I made over 100 videos. On November 6, 1979, I was commended by the commanding officer of the Personnel and Training Bureau for researching, writing, and

Figure 26: In 1980, "Inside LAPD," an 8-minute video covering several topics and distributed throughout the LAPD, with co-host Nancy Dyer and Jeanne Hoover (not photographed).

narrating the training videotape "Controlled Expansion Ammunition." I also started "Inside LAPD," a 10-minute monthly video of four to six subjects hosted on camera by me with Nancy Dyer and, later, Jeanne Hoover. The video encompassed a new law review, tactics, new equipment, and commendable and improper actions by Department personnel, civilian or sworn. Once TVPS completed a video, it had to be approved by the training division commanding officer.

Properly transferring telephone calls from the public to the correct LAPD unit was the subject of a courtesy videotape. The video opened with a woman (my wife) on a floating chair in a swimming pool. A shark was swimming around her. She calls the police. The officer answers her call for help, but instead of listening to what she is saying, the officer concludes the shark is a "loan shark" and incorrectly transfers her call to Bunco-Forgery. The woman is frustrated even more when a detective only listens to part of the story and forwards the call to robbery. The scene ends with only the shark swimming in the pool. Officer Jon Greene from TVP&S directed and produced the videotape. Other TVPS members I worked with included photographers J.D. Caboor and Daniel Martinez and directors Bob Bruggeman, Mike Shane, Frank McGinnis, Jon Greene, and Jim Bultema.

Figure 27: My wife Judy called to report a shark in her pool,
directed by LAPD Officer Jon Greene, in a "Courtesy" video
I wrote for training officers to transfer telephone calls
correctly.

Requests for videos came from throughout the department. For example, an assistant chief of police requested a video about sensitivity and courtesy involving religious groups, especially Hasidic Judaism, in the Hollywood division. As comic relief, the TVPS director and I produced a second video with officers mishandling courtesy. We sent this copy to the commanding officer for approval. Captain Tom Hays, our CO, was shocked at what he saw. Then, the assistant chief came into the office unannounced and wanted to review the video. Unbeknownst to Captain Hays, we switched the video to the correct one and played it for him. Captain Hays squeezed his eyes shut, expecting the Chief's rage. Instead, Captain Hays said he would get even with both of us.

Captain Hays was instrumental in having me join the "Sons of the Desert," the Stan Laurel and Oliver Hardy Fan Club. The club met every other month at a theatre in Hollywood. To be the president and vice president of the club, you had to look like Stan or Ollie. A raffle was held at each meeting, offering memorabilia from their films. Marvin Hatley, who wrote the Cuckoo Song in Laurel and Hardy movies, played the piano while leading the club, singing "We are the Sons of the Desert." The words were,

We are the Sons of the Desert,

Having the time of our lives.

Marching along, two thousand strong,

Far from our sweethearts and wives, God bless them.

Tramp, tramp, tramp the boys are marching, and dancing to this melody,

Sons of the Desert are we.

It was great fun.

During my second year at FTSU, I completed over 50 more scripts and videos and performed on-camera narrations and voiceovers in several recruit training videotapes.

Recruit Training Unit

In 1981, my interest in teaching new officers resulted in my transfer to the Recruit Training Unit for one year. As a result, I became an advisor and instructor for the Recruit Class of March 1981A with advisors Paul Durham, Don Kittridge, and Sergeant Art Ruditsky. My teaching specialty was how to write crime reports.

Creating crime scenes, called "situation simulations," were conducted by instructors to benefit recruit officers to learn how to handle situations in the field. A realistic situation simulation village was atop the police academy, complete with a liquor store, motel, business, sidewalks, and streets. To the rear of each building was a small grandstand so recruits could watch their classmates handle each situation. Instructors posed as victims, witnesses, and suspects. For example, I carried a driver's license named "Ima Senior Citizen, 1150 Nuts Street, Anywhere, CA 95620." Toward the end of the training, the LAPD Special Weapons and Tactics (SWAT) Team conducted situation simulations in the backlots of motion picture studios. These situations used the sounds of gunfire from snipers and armed motorists. Rarely did a recruit survive a crisis yet learn from the experience.

On June 16, 1981, Elysian Park acreage adjacent to the academy was on fire. I organized recruit officers to fight the fire by protecting the grounds surrounding classrooms and other buildings. We were successful, no damage occurred, and no one was injured. We were honored by the Los Angeles Police Revolver and Athletic Club and the Department.

Los Angeles Olympic Games Training Sub-Committee

In 1982, the Olympic Games Planning Group began planning for the 1984 Summer Olympics in Los Angeles. My commanding officer loaned me to the Training Sub Committee. I served on the committee with Los Angeles Sheriff's Department Lieutenant Larry Waldie and U.S. Coast Guard Lieutenant Janice Kirkpatrick. The three of us composed the "Olympic Master Operations Manual," used by staff officers and watch commanders in all seven counties in California staging the Olympics. In addition, we compiled a pocket-sized "Olympic Law Enforcement Handbook," distributed to over 40,000 law enforcement officers during the games. The handbook covered a wide range of subjects, including what to do if an athlete wants to ask for political asylum, how to handle a terrorist threat, and how to make notifications regarding an incident involving the transportation of athletes. We also produced a series of terrorism awareness videotapes narrated by famed actor William Conrad.

During the Olympics, I was the communications monitor assigned to the Olympic Security Coordination Center located in the Ramirez Building downtown. The "war room," or security headquarters, was in action 24 hours a day throughout the Olympics with 52 federal, state, and local law enforcement, government, and military agencies represented. Atop the building was a helicopter pad wherein President Ronald Reagan landed aboard "Marine One." I got to peek inside his helicopter.

Figure 28: Taking a look inside President
Reagan's helicopter "Marine One."

I was also a part of the Olympics Historical Recovery Team, wherein a video cameraman, a still photographer, a sound recording man, and I traveled to each Olympic venue and the Olympic Village, videotaping, and photographing law enforcement in action. Later, we produced videotapes for the Calgary Winter Olympics and future Olympic games.

On August 8, 1984, the Chairman of the Training Subcommittee for the Games, Lieutenant Nick Bakay, commended me for my superb efforts in planning, developing, coordinating, and disseminating training for the Olympic Games. "Your ability to interact well with members of all ranks and to work with various agencies has been an asset. You are always punctual, friendly to work with, and never lack initiative and imagination, regardless of the assignment. You are a true professional."

On June 1, 1985, LAPD Chief of Police Daryl F. Gates commended me for the professional way I performed duties regarding the training process contributed significantly to the fruition of the Summer Games. "Your dedication and diligence resulted in many truly remarkable training aids. The videotapes on Terrorism Awareness, Olympic Orientation, Olympic Security Operations, Consular Relations, and Accreditation were extremely informative and well thought-out. Your work on the Olympic Law Enforcement Handbook and the Olympic Master Operations Manual contributed to absolutely peerless products. Both have received favorable comments from throughout the world. I am extremely proud of your accomplishments. Your work is a credit to the Department and the City of Los Angeles. Thank you for a job well done."

Chapter 8

USC, The Spirit of Troy, and UCLA

September 24, 1977 was my introduction to announcing USC football at the Coliseum as the Trojans defeated the Texas Christian University Horned Frogs 51-0. Over the next 12 years, I substituted for John Ramsey on several occasions, including the Trojans' defeat of the Oregon Ducks 33-15 on October 15, 1977, and Utah State, 66-10 on September 16, 1989. From 1990 through 2012, I was the full-time voice of the Trojans. In 1999, Brendan Loy of the Daily Trojan newspaper wrote, "For fans at the Coliseum, his voice is unmistakable. It is the voice that makes every announcement, explains every penalty, and calls every play. On Saturday, it was the voice that told USC fans to stay off the playing field, and once they were on it, fueled their celebration by declaring the Trojans "city champions" after they defeated UCLA 17-7 for the first time in almost a decade."

Ygnacio Nanetti/The Register

Figure 29: July 20, 1985, the Orange County Register, Dave Strenge wrote an article, "Packer's as good as his words – PA announcer often is confused with Ramsey." John Ramsey is pictured on the right.

John Ramsey

John Jules Ramsey was a living legend, born on July 26, 1927. Until his death on January 25, 1990, from a heart attack, he was the public address announcer for about every professional and collegiate team in Los Angeles. John started announcing at El Camino Junior College in Alondra Park, CA, while attending school. John earned bachelor's and master's degrees from USC. John served in the U.S. Navy and is buried at Riverside National Cemetery.

Figure 30: April 7, 1977, John Ramsey introduces the Dodger's new manager, Tommy Lasorda during opening day at Dodger Stadium.

John's earliest position as the stadium announcer for the new team in town was the former Brooklyn Dodgers, now Los Angeles Dodgers, on April 18, 1958, at the Los Angeles Coliseum. It was also Vin Scully's first Dodger broadcast. John used a hand-held megaphone from a seat behind the home plate area to a crowd of over 78,000. John was the voice for the Angels, Dodgers, Kings, Lakers, Raiders, Aztecs, Rams, USC Trojans, two Super Bowls, 1959, 1967, and 1980 Major League Baseball All-Star Games, the 1984 Olympics, seven World Series, 10 NBA Finals, and the 1963 and 1972 NBA All-Star Games, and several voiceovers in motion pictures. John had an articulate, deliberate, and unruffled announcing style, which I emulated.

An Announcer Is Only as Good as His Spotters

Announcing any sport, especially football, requires knowing the names, numbers, and positions of every player on both teams and the game's rules. I have always said, "An announcer is only as good as his spotters." I have been extremely fortunate to have a cadre of knowledgeable spotters who volunteer to assist me every season. An announcer only has a few seconds to announce what happens during each play and must be accurate at all times. Spotters provide statistics, who the players are on the field, who makes plays, and who makes tackles, and give this information to me while I watch the officials and the action on the field. On September 15, 1990, against Penn State, my spotters were Bob Richert, George Taylorson, and Joe De Ladurantey.

Figure 31: USC Spotters from left to right: George Taylorson, Bob Richert, me, and Joe De Ladurantey.

My spotters come from various professions. My other spotters for USC, UCLA, and both games included George L. Throop III, Brent Ferguson, Steve Gillespie, Robin Mahkorn, Nick Rose, Gaylord "Bud" Grover, Tom O'Brien, and Jonathan Horowitz.

I became acquainted with this exceptional young man, Jonathan Horowitz, in 2005. He was a journalism major at USC and wrote several articles about me in The Daily Trojan. Jonathan also expressed an interest in becoming a public address announcer. I did what I could to assist him, and he accomplished his wish in more ways than one. Jonathan is the track announcer at Bally's Arapahoe horse racetrack in Aurora, Colorado, and broadcasts for the Arabian Jockey Club at the Saudi Cup in Saudi Arabia. In addition, Jonathan is the men's and women's basketball, lacrosse, hockey, volleyball, and gymnastics announcer at the University of Denver. He also announces horse shows for the U.S. Eventing Association. In addition, he flies to California to help spot at NFLPA Collegiate All-Star Games.

USC Trojans Football

USC home game days were memorable. My spotters and I carpooled to the Coliseum from Arcadia. After breakfast at a local restaurant, we headed to Cromwell Field on the USC campus for band practice. My spotters loved it when the band director, Dr. Arthur C. Bartner, yelled at me during rehearsal. Next, we drove over to the press parking lot. We stopped at several tailgate parties on our way to the press box elevator. We would see and talk to former USC coach and quarterback Craig Fertig, USC radio broadcaster Tom Kelly, LAPD Captain Ed Brown, and former LAPD Chief of Police Daryl F. Gates. The best tailgaters of all were Robert and Kristina Sonheim. Robert's pregame cooking was excellent, especially his fried onions.

In the press box, our first stop was one of the most excellent people you would ever want to meet, now retired, USC Sports Information Director Tim Tessalone, who provided me with game information, statistics, and other information. The next stop was programs and additional information from Lee and Valerie Sampson, who ran the press box with Richard Lopez and several other gracious individuals. Then, a stop by the USC radio broadcast booth and one of the greatest announcers around, Pete

Arbogast, and his spotters Bert Iwata and Mark Hoppe, for player names pronunciations and other information.

During USC home games, while I was concentrating on announcements and the game, the Yell Leaders shot hacky sack balls into the stands. One hit me right in the nose, yet I continued announcing without missing a word. My spotter, Bob Richert, awarded me a plaque holding the hacky sack with the terms, "In light of your coolness under fire... the undersigned declared if an artillery barrage occurred, they wanted me by their sides."

The Spirit of Troy

In 1988, I became acquainted with "The Man on the Ladder" Dr. Emeritus Arthur C. Bartner, Director of "Hollywood's Band," The Spirit of Troy, the USC Trojan Marching Band, "the greatest college band in the history of the universe," as their pregame and halftime announcer. Over the next 23 seasons, Art and his wife Barbara became close friends with my wife Judy and me. My wife and I traveled with the band to London, England, Shanghai, China, and numerous bowl games and Notre Dame.

Figure 32: My wife Judy and I traveled with
the Spirit of Troy and Art and Barbara
Bartner to faraway places like Shanghai,
China.

Every Thursday before a USC home game, I would meet Art for lunch, and he would outline the upcoming pregame and halftime shows, so I could write a script and read it at games. On Saturday mornings, I attended dress rehearsals for the shows on the USC campus and met with Dr. Tony Fox, who arranged the band's music. I learned early on to make my announcements timely. If I picked the wrong signal, I got yelled at by Dr. Bartner, just like band members who played the wrong note at the wrong time. Fortunately, I never had to take a lap like band members who made mistakes. I also traveled with the band to announce their shows at away games at Stanford University in Palo Alto, the University of California at Berkeley, the University of Notre Dame, and bowl games throughout the U.S. Art liked having a police officer by his side.

On January 1, 2008, the Trojans played the University of Illinois at the 94th Rose Bowl. During pregame, the band stands at attention on the sideline. Then, the USC Drum Major struts along the 50-yard line to the center of the field and stabs the ground with his sword. He then waves his sword to the Trojan Marching Band, who responds, "Beat the Illini," which is my cue to start announcing:

"Ladies and gentlemen. Presenting the Spirit of Troy, the University of Southern California, Trojan Marching Band. Band, take the field."

The band then steps off, and I say:

"With Drum Major Daniel Lickman and twirlers Elyssa Espinosa, Kim Boynton, and Emily Clapper."

At the end of playing the Tribute to Troy, I say:

"Celebrating the Trojans' unprecedented 6th consecutive PAC-10 title, and 3rd trip to the Rose Bowl, here is the Spirit of Troy with, "All Right Now," featuring the world-famous U-S-C Song Girls."

At the end of "All Right Now", after the applause, fanfare begins, and I say:

"And now, collegiate football's greatest battle cry, CONQUEST."

Trojan's mascot, Traveler (horse), enters the field and rears up; I say:

"And, the Trojan's mascot, Traveler, ridden by Hector Aguilar."

Band halts and then leaves the field, and I say:`` University of Southern California, Trojan Marching Band."

The University of Notre Dame Fighting Irish

Traveling with the band to Notre Dame was always a memorable experience. My first of 11 whirlwind trips to Notre Dame with the USC Trojan Marching Band were on October 28, 1989. Every other year, the Spirit of Troy, with over 300 members and support personnel, travels for four days, from take-off on Thursday at Los Angeles International Airport to Chicago. Then, on Friday mornings at 6:00 am, sometimes as many as six chartered buses and a large truck delivered the band and instruments to a local Chicago high school athletic field. First, the band warmed up and practiced the pregame and halftime shows for the game on Saturday. Then despite the inclement weather and freezing temperatures, the band played on.

The high schoolers were thrilled to watch the band practice. Then, after rehearsal and putting on their uniforms, they ate a box lunch on their way to the Navy Pier for a pep rally. The rallies attracted

Figure 33: With the USC Marching Band on the field after the game with Spirit Troy assistant director/arranger Dr. Tony Fox.

thousands of USC alums, fans, and Chicagoans. After an afternoon break, the band played another pep rally at a downtown Chicago hotel sponsored by USC Alumni. Saturday was the game as we traveled for several hours across Illinois to South Bend, Indiana. A police escort led us to a University of Notre Dame practice facility. The Notre Dame fans were warm, friendly, and excited to see the band. Ironically, Ken Dye is the Director of the Notre Dame Fighting Irish Marching Band. He acquired his music experience while attending college at USC, where he played the trombone with the Spirit of Troy. After another dress rehearsal, the band marched across campus to the stadium. I headed to the press box to announce pregame and halftime.

I also developed friendships with several Notre Dame individuals. First was Mike Collins, the game announcer from 1981-2020. Mike was also a reporter, producer, news director, and news anchor for WNDU-TV and WSBT-TV in South Bend.

Figure 34: Notre Dame stadium announcer Mike Collins and Indiana State Trooper Sergeant Tim McCarthy.

I sat in Mike's booth and spotted USC during games. The second person was Indiana State Trooper Sergeant Tim McCarthy, who read a humorous safety message at the end of the 3rd quarter of every home game.

While exploring the press box, I mistakenly entered a room where several priests enjoyed the game. They welcomed me to sit with them and enjoy a Hot Toddy. The thing I will really miss is the homemade soup served in the press box.

The Cardinal and the Bears

During eleven of the Spirit of Troy's alternate weekend travels to Stanford University and the University of California at Berkeley, I developed a friendship with the Bears marching band pregame and halftime announcer, Sacramento Assistant District Attorney Albert Locher. Most of the Cardinal and Bears games were on the same weekend as the Raiders or Chargers games, so I had to rush from the press box after halftime to the airport to fly home in time for the Sunday games.

Japan Bowl

From 1989-1993, I was honored to be the stadium announcer for the Japan Bowl played in January in Yokohama, Japan. The game featured the top collegiate players and coaches from around the U.S. The event included a nine-day trip to Tokyo and surrounding cities. During the 1989 trip, Emperor Hirohito died, and the nation was in mourning. Many stores and museums were closed, so I wandered around Tokyo and discovered the largest fish market in the world, the Tsukiji Market, a two-mile square area filled with fish and eating places. I was astonished at the variety of fish-Eels, octopuses, sharks, crabs, and tuna. Auctioneers barked prices to representatives from cruise lines and hotels who were the biggest customers. The market opened at 3:00 am and closed at 9:00 am.

When I returned to the hotel, several players asked where I had been, and I told them about the fish market. They convinced me to lead them to the fish market the next day. Unbeknownst to me, in honor of the passing of the emperor, the fish market was closed the next day for the first time. Well, we got up early and took the subway to the market. Unfortunately, and to my surprise, the marketplace was closed. Can you imagine seeing a disserted marketplace? I looked at those giant football players and disgruntled Tennessee head coach Johnny Majors and thought I would never live this experience down. The Japan Bowl staff got a big laugh. Fortunately, the next day, players and coaches went to the market and saw what I saw.

At one game, I was really thirsty and asked the Japan Bowl media representative for some water. He returned with a beverage in a can and said this would quench your thirst. I drank it and thought it to be lukewarm, but it did quench my thirst. When I got a translation of what was in the can, that made me feel really mellow, it was sake.

In 1994, I had a conflict with my day job. So, I reached out to Public Address Announcer Robert Bruce "Bink" Binkowski, the stadium announcer for the San Diego Padres and San Diego Chargers, to see if he was available to announce the Japan Bowl that year. He jumped at the chance and did a great job.

Motion Picture Voiceovers

My affiliation with The Spirit of Troy led to me performing voiceovers in three motion pictures as a day player. First, on July

19, 1988, Paramount Pictures had me act as the baseball public address announcer in "The Naked Gun: From the Files of Police Squad," a hilarious comedy about an assassin trying to kill the Queen of England on her visit to Los Angeles. Driving through Paramount Picture's main entrance to a soundstage for the voiceover was exciting. On one wall, a screen showed clips of the movie where voiceovers or sounds were supposed to be. A traffic light just below the screen indicated a red, yellow, and green light signaling the actor to begin reading their script. While waiting in the outer office and studying my lines, I listened while an actor performed "crying and whimpering" inside the soundstage. The actor's crying and whimpering were to be overlayed over actor George Kennedy, portraying a detective, to whimper and cry while witnessing a steam roller and the USC Marching Band run-over actor Ricardo Monteban's body outside Dodger Stadium. The "crying" actor took several hours to record. I had over 35 lines to read, worried it would take hours to do all my lines. When the actor finished, I went onto the soundstage.

My opening line was, "Ladies and gentlemen. On behalf of the California Angels and the City of Los Angeles, on behalf of her majesty's royal visit, please rise for our National Anthem performed by renowned opera star Enrico Pallazzo." The line was funny because the game was taking place at Dodgers Stadium, and actor Leslie Neilson played the part of a detective who hog-tied the real Enrico Pallazzo so he would be in a position to identify who was going to kill the Queen. Another line was, "Ladies and gentlemen, let us honor America as Mr. Pallazzo will sing our National Anthem." Then, after the Queen of England was introduced to toss out the first ball, another line was, "How about that Queen, Ladies and gentlemen? Let's have a nice round of applause." I went through the rest of the lines without a hitch and finished after just one hour. I was proud of myself. As I reentered the outer office, the crying actor asked me if I was new to the business of acting. I replied I was. He said they pay you by the hour ($398), so each time you work, take your time to finish.

My second voiceover was on July 3, 1990, in Hollywood Picture Company's "Filofax, aka Taking Care of Business," a comedy about a professional thief who escapes from jail and uses someone else's identity and date book to go to the World Series in style. The World Series was at Anaheim Stadium, with the California Angels, who had never been to the World Series, versus the Chicago Cubs, who had not been to the World Series since 1908. Again, I had over 30 lines in the movie that went without a hitch, yet I still finished in one hour ($431).

My third voiceover as a day performer was on November 6, 1991, in Warner Bros Inc., "The Last Boy Scout," about a former secret service agent who is a private investigator investigating a murder and a football player with a gambling problem, bribery, and legalizing sports gambling. My role was the stadium announcer for professional football played in the rain at the Los Angeles Memorial Coliseum. Again, I had over 30 lines in the movie that went without a hitch but took several hours. This time, I looked forward to receiving a healthy paycheck but discovered that because this was my third movie, the Taft-Hartley Act required I join the Screen Actors Guild. Unfortunately, the membership cost ate up my $448 multiple hours pay. The one redeeming aspect was that I would receive residuals from my voiceover day performer work in the three movies. Today, I joked at receiving a six-cent residual check for video screenings of a film.

Other USC Sports and Activities

During the second half of the USC basketball 1991 season, I announced the games for ailing announcer George Harris. After that, I announced USC basketball through 2000. I also announced USC's Women of Troy basketball games and gymnastics tournaments.

At the Cerritos Center for the Performing Arts, I was the background announcer for the Trojan Marching Band's annual Spring Concerts.

UCLA Bruins Football and Basketball

On March 7, 1990, Stephen S. Salm, UCLA Athletic Department Associate Director, sent me a letter of appreciation for announcing a tribute to staff members who had worked at Pauley Pavilion for 25 years. He stated my performance was flawless and the quality of my voice was marvelous. One of the volunteers honored was my Monroe High School basketball coach Bill Rankin.

In June 1992, months before the start of the 1992 college football season, I got a telephone call from UCLA Sports Information Director Marc Dellins. Marc stated that long-time UCLA stadium announcer Don Sawyer suffered from an illness and was unavailable to announce the upcoming UCLA football at the Rose Bowl and basketball games at Pauley Pavilion on the UCLA campus. Marc asked if I could fill in until UCLA could find a replacement. Because I was already the USC football announcer, I contacted USC Sports Information Director Tim Tessalone and Athletic Director Mike McGee to seek their permission. They responded that USC had reservations about me serving as the announcer at both USC and UCLA football games because I was their signature voice-out for the fans. They also wanted me to prioritize USC when there were conflicting games. As a result, there was only one possible conflict during the entire season. My contract with UCLA started on September 1, 1992, and ended on March 30, 1993.

Figure 35: Announcing UCLA Bruins football with Spotters George Taylorson, Tom O'Brien, and Steve Gillespie.

On October 10, 1992, the USC Trojans would play the University of Oregon Ducks at the Coliseum, with the kickoff at 3:30 pm. The game ended at 6:35 pm. Then, at 7:00 pm., the UCLA Bruins would play the Stanford Cardinal at the Rose Bowl. So how would I go from the Coliseum to the Rose Bowl to announce both games? The answer was a helicopter. A helicopter pilot friend of mine picked me up atop the Seeley G. Mudd Building on the USC campus and landed at the Pasadena Police Department helicopter pad adjacent to the Rose Bowl. From there, the police drove me to the Rose Bowl in time to announce the UCLA game. After that, the season went off without a hitch. During the UCLA vs. USC game at the Rose

Bowl on November 21, 1992, UCLA Head Coach Terry Donahue and USC Head Coach Larry Smith stated they could not tell which team I was rooting for in my announcements.

John R. Wooden Classic

From December 1994 through 2002, I announced the John R. Wooden Classic collegiate basketball invitational at the Arrowhead Pond of Anaheim. The one-day, two-basketball game invitational, played back-to-back, showcased four outstanding teams from throughout the U.S., USC, and UCLA. It was incredibly challenging because I had to memorize all four teams' names and numbers without making any mistakes. In the first game, Pepperdine University played the UCLA Bruins. Twenty minutes after the first game's conclusion, the University of Kansas Jayhawks played Oklahoma State University Cowboys. By the end of the second game, I was mentally exhausted. Thereafter, I announced the Wooden Classic for eight years.

Rose Bowl Games

On New Year's Day 1997 (83rd Rose Bowl - Arizona State v. Ohio State), 1998 (84th Rose Bowl - Washington State v. Michigan), 1999 (85th Rose Bowl - UCLA v. Wisconsin), and 2000 (86th Rose Bowl - Stanford v. Wisconsin), I was the stadium announcer for the games in Pasadena.

Figure 36: Announcing the Rose Bowl with Spotters Bob Richert, George Taylorson, and George L. Throop III.

My spotters were George L. Throop III, Bob Richert, George Taylorson, Joe De Ladurantey, and Brent Ferguson.

December 31, 1999, I was the announcer for the Rose Bowl Game Kickoff Luncheon and Hall of Fame. I also announced the coronation of the 2000 Tournament of Roses' queen and court.

Whenever the Trojans played in bowl games, I announced pregame, and halftime shows for the Spirit of Troy. The bowl games included Michigan State in the 1990 John Hancock Bowl, Texas Tech in the 1995 Cotton Bowl, Northwestern in the 1996 Rose Bowl, Michigan in the 2004 Rose Bowl, Texas in the 2006 Rose Bowl, Michigan in the 2007 Rose Bowl, and Illinois in the 2008 Rose Bowl.

"Packer's Departure Leaves a Void"

After the 2012 USC football season, members of the athletic department decided to discontinue my announcing games and the band. They chose a new announcer, Eric Smith, who had been my backup announcer for the Clippers. Joey Kaufman with the Daily Trojan wrote, "Packer's Departure Leaves a Void. There doesn't seem to be an explanation, not an adequate one anyway." The athletic department issued a press release on its website stating that auditions were part of an "ongoing effort to update the football game day experience... and looking into the possibility of a new voice to usher in the latest era of USC football." Because of the vagueness, Kaufman asked a school spokesman for more information. "After all, 22-year employees don't typically disappear—not without at least saying some goodbye or farewell."

October 30, 2021, I was invited back to the Coliseum for a special halftime salute to Professor Emeritus Dr. Arthur C. Bartner and his 51 years of service to the University of Southern California, a definitive legacy. I announced at halftime as nearly 1,200 Spirit of Troy musicians, drum majors, twirlers, S.C. Silks, and USC Song Girls, representing 50 years of great Trojan Marching Band alums, paid tribute to Dr. Bartner.

Chapter 9

Narcotics Division

Following the 1984 Summer Olympic Games in Los Angeles, I wanted a different kind of staff writing job and sought a position in Narcotics Division. Although the war on drugs started in the early 1970s, drug trafficking in southern California really began to take off in the 1980s.

Staff Services Unit

On March 30, 1986, I got transferred from the Training Division to a plainclothes assignment in the Narcotics Division, Staff Services Unit, as a staff writer. I researched narcotics-related subjects, authored a sensitive corruption prevention program, analyzed new laws, and prepared press releases. Supervised by Lieutenant Elmer A. "JR" Schiller and Detective III Mike Celmer, it was an enviable position because I got to leave the office and respond to major seizures of drugs and money wherever they happened and then brief command staff for upcoming press conferences.

Narcotics Division also consisted of detectives working as Major Violators Section targeting major drug traffickers; the Field Enforcement Section targeting drug dealers in the 22 geographic divisions of the LAPD; and specialized units, including the Clandestine Lab Squad targeting illicit drug manufacturing; NIN (Narcotics Information Network) keeping tabs on narcotics investigations throughout the LAPD; Airport Details at Los Angeles International Airport and Ontario International Airport targeting drug and money couriers; K-9s for drug detection city-wide; and Electronics Detail handling the installation of surveillance equipment.

One of my most interesting assignments was doing research and writing for an LAPD-wide Corruption Prevention Program. Uniformed police officers and plainclothes detectives are exposed daily to contraband and entrusted with handling illicit drugs and millions of dollars of cash. In developing this new program, I researched police corruption investigations in New York City, Miami, and New Orleans. The most common factor I found in police corruption cases was the lack of supervision of sworn and civilian police personnel handling illicit drugs and money. I did not know it then, but the project would contribute to my handling of financial investigations and money laundering of alleged major corruption by police officers, detectives, supervision, department staff and public officials. My Commanding Officer, Captain III Robert J. Blanchard, commended me for the work I did in putting it together, "Your work on the corruption prevention program was exemplary, thoroughly researched, well-written, and organized. This effort will have far-reaching consequences as the program becomes the very solid foundation upon which to maintain the integrity of this Department."

Two of the new laws I was excited about analyzing were Section 11470 of the California Penal Code, and Title 21 United States Code Section 881(a), Asset Forfeiture. The laws enabled law enforcement officers to seize real and/or personal property furnished or intended to be furnished in exchange for a controlled substance, or certain types of property used or intended to be used to facilitate certain crimes and, in some instances, specific amounts of controlled substances, or all property with its proceeds traceable to an exchange of a controlled substance. The asset seized is the guilty party. "Standing" meant who had an interest in the asset. An asset could be money, bank accounts, stocks, investments, automobiles, trucks, boats, aircraft, real estate, or anything of intrinsic value. Finding out who the asset belonged to was the fun part. Investigating suspect statements and actions; statements made by others, including attorneys and witnesses; researching every aspect of a seizure; and writing search and seizure orders were always fascinating. A forfeiture investigation was like a box of chocolates; you never know what you are going to get. A simple seizure of money or a vehicle could lead investigators to a major trafficking organization. Asset forfeiture cases could occur locally, nationally, or in another part of the world. The time limit on a state case was one year, whereas federal cases could go on for years.

Financial investigations have a three-fold impact on criminals and criminal organizations: first, financial investigations serve as an invaluable tool in narcotics investigations because they uncover the proceeds of crime (money drives criminal enterprises), as well as expose the trail of evidence that leads investigators through the organization and to other co-conspirators; second, financial investigations can result in not only enhancing drug charges but add additional charges for financial related offenses, i.e., racketeering, money laundering, and tax evasion; and third, in addition to filing criminal counts, financial investigations have dismantled criminal enterprises by not only seizing their assets, bail and attorney's fees for forfeiture but by adding financial sanctions by the court during sentencing. Five aspects of a financial investigation are: collection of raw data – by reading the arrest reports and physically looking through, analyzing, and organizing the evidence; writing search warrants; conducting financial interviews, investigators can learn more about the target than they knew before, rebut defenses; and establish or verify facts; understand complex circumstances – a financial investigation will tell you if you are investigating an individual or a drug organization; and expose schemes – the purpose of profit crimes such as drug trafficking, racketeering, corruption, and other financial conspiracies is to generate and use illegal proceeds without detection by financial institutions, law enforcement, and regulatory agencies. These schemes will give the investigator insight into the methodology used by the target, including unusual and unnecessary financial transactions; convoluted and complex money movements; deceptions, false statements, and documents; and secrecy and pretext income screens to hide and spend illegal proceeds without detection; dismantling the drug dealer or enterprise through seizing assets for forfeiture; and make you an all-around investigator.

According to the U.S. Department of the Treasury, "Money is laundered to conceal illegal activity, including the crimes that generate the money itself, such as drug trafficking. Money laundering conceals the source of illegal proceeds so that the money can be used without detection of its criminal source." The three main reasons why criminals, whether they are drug traffickers, organized crime, embezzlers, or involved in corruption, have to launder money is they need to use the money to expand operations, acquire assets, buy power, and improve their standing in the community (power broker); small bills ($1, $2, $5, $10 and $20's) are bulky to handle; and, money itself is vulnerable to rip-offs by competition, theft by their own people, would draw suspicion if used to buy things in large amounts and could be seized by police.

Money laundering involves three different, and sometimes overlapping, stages: the first stage is the placement of money, which involves physically moving illegally obtained money from a direct association with the crime into the financial system or the retail economy. Money is most vulnerable to detection and seizure during placement and may involve the conversion of street cash, the exchange of small denomination bills to $50 and $100 bills, money order or cashier's check, or change the holder from the individual to a financial institution; bulk currency smuggling by moving the money from one point to another or over the U.S. border into a foreign country; structuring is a term used to describe any conduct where a person breaks down large amounts of money, under $10,000, into several deposits, or converts the money to another monetary instrument so as evade the filing of a Currency Transaction Report. The act or acts of doing this is a felony. A financial institution is required by the Bank Secrecy Act to complete a CTR whenever more than $10,000 in cash is deposited, withdrawn, or wire transferred. The CTR is then sent to the Internal Revenue Service for further review. The act of structuring is hopefully accomplished by not drawing suspicion from the financial institution.

In the days before the creation of the CTR, structuring was called "Smurfing." It got this term from the actions of a short Colombian drug trafficker who recruited low-level member(s) of the cartel to fan out throughout the southern states and Florida and structure the conversion of drug dollars into cashier's checks payable to him. They became known as Smurfs because the men were short, like their boss, and resembled Smurf cartoon characters on television. Each worker was paid $50 for each $10,000 check they obtained. The Smurfs converted over $30 million in cash to checks during a two-week run.

The U.S. Department of the Treasury, to detect structuring, created the CTR. A few years after the CTR form was implemented, drug dealers and other criminal enterprises got even more creative in structuring transactions by keeping their deposits under $10,000 with even dollar deposits of $9,900, $9,800, $9,700, and so on. To counteract this activity, the Suspicious Activity Report was created to require the reporting of any transaction over $2,000 and under $10,000 or any activity the bank deemed to be suspicious. Over the years, some drug dealers realized the $9,000 transactions might be risky and lowered the structured amounts around the $3,000 range. The IRS Form 8300, "Report of Cash Payments Over $10,000 Received in a Trade or Business," was created for businesses, such as automobile dealerships, to provide the same information contained in the CTR and SAR.

The second stage is layering. This stage involves engaging in a complex series of secondary transactions designed to further separate criminally obtained proceeds from the original source of funds, making it difficult to trace. For example, a drug organization posing as a recording company opened three bank accounts at three different banks for each of the three fictitious rock bands. As drug money poured in, the money was deposited (structured) in even-dollar amounts into each of the aforementioned accounts, and the owners told bank employees it was from concerts and album sales. The suspects even went to the trouble to give bank employees CD-ROMS, coffee cups, and other items with logos of their company name and the name of the rock bands. Once the money was layered into these accounts, the money was wired to the main company account and then spent on real estate and other investments.

The third stage is integration, which involves making the funds look as if they were legitimately earned. Integration may include the purchase of automobiles, businesses, real estate, etc. The commingling of cash from an illegal source with money from a legitimate enterprise is another example of integration.

Asset Forfeiture Investigative Detail

Shortly after passing the asset forfeiture laws, Narcotics Division created the Asset Forfeiture Investigative Detail with two detectives and a supervisor. Soon thereafter, the seizure of more assets needed a larger office and additional staff support. I remember one Thursday afternoon when everyone was getting ready for a three-day holiday weekend in 1989, a call came in from a citizen who had observed a small pickup truck being unloaded outside a warehouse in Sylmar, a suburb of Los Angeles in the North San Fernando Valley. The citizen further described brick-like shaped packages resembling kilograms of cocaine falling out of the back of the pickup. Hardly any detectives were around, so they recruited some experienced AFID detectives to respond to the warehouse to further investigate. Upon arrival, the truck was gone. They then peered through a window in the door and observed boxes stacked in the warehouse with unusual markings that had words scribbled on the sides of the boxes in Spanish, translated as "100 kilos," and boxes labeled '$$$'.

Thinking about the warehouse and boxes might contain contraband, the detectives obtained a search warrant and entered the warehouse. They then discovered pallet-sized boxes containing cash and cocaine. It took several days to count the money. The count turned out to be over $19.8 million. Shortly thereafter, the AFID was expanded to over 25 personnel, including a lieutenant, supervisors, 10 investigators, and 4 support personnel. The department was renamed to the Financial Unit. I wanted to be a part of the unit and transferred to it on May 1, 1987. I had no idea this would be the best career move I had ever made, and I remained there for the next 19 years. I was promoted to Detective and Detective Supervisor until I retired on June 30, 2008.

My first assignment was maintaining conveyances (mainly automobiles) seized by LAPD narcotics detectives. Cars and trucks, including big rigs (tractor-trailers), in state investigations, were stored in a secret warehouse near Union Station in downtown Los Angeles. Seizures of vehicles from federal investigations were stored by the United States Marshals Service at a warehouse in the City of Commerce. The state cases were stored in 'secret' because many of the vehicles were luxury cars, including a Ferrari Testarossa, a Lamborghini, Chevrolet Corvettes, and pricey foreign automobiles. State and federal laws required vehicles to be in the condition wherein they were seized. I had to drive these vehicles around town and even home and keep them clean until the disposition of a particular case in court. My neighbors were beginning to think I was shady driving so many different exotic vehicles home.

Years later, an LAPD commander went to the warehouse with an L.A. Times photographer and posed with the exotic cars for a story entitled "Car Czar." After the release of the story, the next night, the warehouse was broken into, and several items, including stereos, speakers, and parts, were stolen from the vehicles. I remember one day; I got a call from a special agent in Miami. He inquired about the disposition of a big rig seized in an investigation conducted jointly by the Drug Enforcement Administration agents and the LAPD. I knew there was no big rig in the warehouse and called the U.S. Marshals to see if they had stored the big rig. They did not, and so I called the special agent back, reporting no big rig was found. He said, in federal court, the big rig was awarded to the DEA in Miami. I then called the detectives who initiated the seizure in the first place. One of the detectives told me the big rig was parked near the secret warehouse on a side street. I then drove to the side street and found the big rig with flat tires and parking tickets on the windshield dating back to the seizure. I called the special agent back, and the case was solved. I was thankful when detectives opened the back door of the trailer and did not find any cash or contraband.

In another investigation, Major Violators Section detectives intercepted a van leaving the beach in National City, California, containing hundreds of kilograms of cocaine. During the investigation, nine suspects were arrested and prosecuted federally. Detectives found the cocaine came from a boat that traveled from Mexico off the National City coastline and then dumped on the beach. While inventorying the van for asset forfeiture, I observed sand in the rear of the van. I swept the sand into a zip lock bag and placed it with the case file. Later, the baggie of sand was delivered to the Scientific Investigation Division for analysis. The analysis found that the sand originated from the beach at National City. The defendants said that they were nowhere near the beach. During the federal trial, I was called to testify about the sand. It turned out the sand was a crucial element in placing the defendants at the beach and contributed to their conviction.

I was also partnered with more experienced detectives in the Financial Unit for training purposes. These detectives included Robert "Bob" Gartner, Tommy Thompson, Jim Day, Jim Dumelle, and William "Bill Scharfen. In one of my earliest cases in 1988, a large amount of cash was seized from a drug dealer in Carson, CA. The dealer was also the leader of a cocaine trafficking group since 1986, consisting of more than 40 individuals. His BMW had a personalized license plate, "FREAKS," which turned out to be the name of his organization. During the service of a search warrant at his home by Narcotics Division Majors, I could not help but notice the master bedroom closet was filled with hundreds of shoe boxes containing various brands of expensive athletic shoes.

He was also a cargo employee for a major airline. The investigation showed he would place suitcases full of cocaine in one of the baggage holds in a passenger jet. Airlines were allowed to carry up to 3,000 pounds of company cargo not subject to inspection by anyone except the airline. Planes carrying suitcases of cocaine were on flights to Dallas, Texas; Atlanta, Georgia; Memphis, Nashville; Chattanooga, Tennessee; and Birmingham, Alabama. Flight attendants would then carry the bags to a particular individual at each airport, who would then deliver the bags to street dealers for distribution. Suitcases full of cash would then be transported back to Los Angeles using cargo holds. The flight attendants, for their assistance, were treated to spending sprees at jewelry stores in destination cities and Los Angeles.

One of the handlers was apprehended in Chattanooga by federal agents. While in custody, the handler chose to confess his role in the organization and how the cocaine was distributed to minimize his sentencing in federal court. I, along with two MVS detectives handling the investigation, went to Birmingham, Alabama, to debrief the handler. During the interview, I felt he was not truthful and gave us the information we already knew about the case. In the courtroom, the federal judge asked us about the interview. We told him the handler was uncooperative and did not give us any new information. The judge then had the defendant face him in court. The judge told him the detectives came all the way from California to interview him and give him a chance to have his sentence reduced. "...since you did not cooperate, I could have sentenced you to a much lower sentence, I am sentencing you today to 40 years in the Atlanta Federal Penitentiary."

I looked at the defendant, and he was in shock and disbelief as he was ushered out of the courtroom by the bailiffs. Later, I would learn, that he told federal agents everything about the Freaks, their contacts in the organization, their cocaine connection in Mexico, and the flight attendants involved.

Another almost disastrous scenario involved the seizure of a 50-foot yacht off the California Coast near Oxnard, California. The luxurious yacht was used by drug traffickers to sail 40 miles off the coast and meet up with a trawler to receive shipments of cocaine. Early in the morning, Financial Unit detectives responded to Oxnard to assist other detectives with the seizure of the yacht. The two detectives, claiming they had sailing experience, volunteered to sail the yacht from Oxnard to the Port of Los Angeles to a storage slip used by the U.S Marshals Service and called their supervisor to advise him of their plan. They assured him that it would only take approximately four hours to sail the yacht from Oxnard to the harbor. At 5 pm, I got a telephone call from one of the wives of the two detectives, wanting to know when she could expect him home. Back in those days, we did not have cellular phones. We had pagers. I paged them but knew unless the yacht had a radio that they could use to answer the page, I would not hear from them.

Meanwhile, back on the yacht, the two detectives thought they would follow the coastline down to the harbor. While using the boat motor instead of sailing, they discovered the yacht was equipped with a complete wet bar and sampled some of the libations. Then they got sleepy and took a nap. When they awoke, it was nighttime, and they could not see the lights along the coastline and did not know that they were headed directly west, out to sea. The next morning, I got another phone call from one of the wives, but this time she sounded very concerned. I was speechless and asked my supervisor if he had heard from the detectives. He had not, and so we called the Marshals and then the U.S. Coast Guard. The Coast Guard reported that they had eyes on the wayward yacht; it was 250 nautical miles heading west. The Coast Guard came to the rescue and guided the yacht to the harbor later that day. The two detectives, upon returning to their office, asked for overtime and were sent on their merry way. The story does not end here.

The next day, another officer, who was now the keeper of seized conveyances and boats, drove down to the harbor to inspect the yacht and take inventory of everything on it. While conducting the inspection, the officer wanted to turn on the radar, fish finder, and radio to check their condition. He then realized the only way to turn on the power was to start the engines on the yacht. Before the engines would start, plugs on either side of the aft had to be removed so water could circulate and cool the engines. After inspecting all the gadgetry, the officer turned off the engines, locked the cabin, and went back to the office. The next day, the officer told us all about the yacht and all its expensive contents. We then decided to go down to the harbor and check the yacht out ourselves. Upon arrival, the yacht was nowhere to be seen. A harbor employee told us the yacht was not gone. We decided to look down into the water and could just barely see the mast. The officer forgot to put the plugs back into the aft of the yacht, so it took on water overnight and eventually sank. Later, it would take a U.S. Navy crane to lift the yacht to the surface. Fortunately, the yacht was forfeited to the feds, so the officer who pulled the plugs was not charged with re-conditioning the yacht, which could have cost over $5,000.

Chapter 10

"Convoluted" Is Putting It Mildly

Though asset forfeiture may begin as a civil investigation, it could eventually become criminal. Remember, the guilty party is the asset or assets seized for forfeiture. The investigation involves determining "standing," which means who has "an interest" in the asset seized. All statements made by the person(s) to whom the asset(s) was seized are admissible in a court of law. As a result, some of the explanations regarding seized assets were at times convoluted and sometimes unbelievable. This next case is one of the most unusual and unbelievable investigations.

In November 1989, the West Bureau Buy Team officers received information from citizens that illicit drugs were being sold from a house in the 1300 block of South Orange Grove, Los Angeles. An arrest was made in front of the house, and it was apparent the house was a hangout for street gang members. Officers also learned the house was owned by a woman and her son, who also lived in the house. On January 23, 1990, a citizen complained to the area city councilman that the house was a hangout for street gangs and the selling of illicit drugs. On February 7, 1990, police learned the house was the territory of the "By Yourself Hustlers," a known Black street gang.

Detectives from MVS received information from an informant of a trafficking group in the Wilshire District of Los Angeles who wanted to purchase 10 kilograms of cocaine. On March 21, 1990, detectives arranged a "reverse sting," wherein undercover detectives posing as drug traffickers "fronted" 10 kilograms of cocaine to the traffickers. Thereafter, the traffickers fronted the money to pay for the cocaine, approximately $325,000, in the trunk of a 1988 Honda Accord, 4-door, maroon in color, driven by a female. Unbeknownst to the traffickers, other plainclothes detectives followed the car with the cash away from the front location and had uniformed officers in a black and white police vehicle do a traffic stop of the car. The officers approached the female driver and asked her to look in her trunk. She obliged, and the officers observed the bundles of cash. When asked about the money, the driver replied that she did not know anything about it. The California Health and Safety Code enables law enforcement to arrest a person for a felony who is in possession of $100,000 or more of unexplained cash or denies ownership of the money connected to illegal drugs. She was then arrested, and the currency was seized pursuant to Asset Forfeiture. The detectives then contacted the Financial Unit for assistance. I was assigned the case. During a count of the money, it was found that several telephone book yellow pages had been trimmed to the exact size of dollar bills and inserted into the bundles. The actual count totaled $304,895 and not $325,000.

On March 29, 1990, I received a phone call from a woman stating that the 1988 Honda Accord belonged to two women who lived in Washington, D.C., and loaned the car to a man who loaned the car to the female with the money. Shortly thereafter, I received a telephone call from an attorney, who said he was handling the case for the female. However, the charge against the female was not filed.

On April 9, 1990, the same attorney called me and said he was not representing the female anymore and was now representing another client who was claiming the seized currency. The attorney said the money meant investment money from unknown sources. I then asked for a conference with the attorney and his client.

On April 11, 1990, I met with the attorney and his client, this time a male identifying himself as a preacher, at the attorney's office in Santa Monica. My partner, Detective Jim Dumelle, accompanied me to the meeting. At the conference, the male, who was wearing a preacher's collared shirt, said he was the Assistant Minister of a Baptist Church in South Central Los Angeles where he performed sermons and funerals. He said he was paid $250 for sermons and $150 for funerals. He stated that he is also a toy inventor and manufacturer. Besides preaching, he stated he earned extra money creating toys since 1985 for children. The name of his business was called, "Flying High Products by Wilson." He stated he earned $35,000 per month in gross sales and $420,000 per year. He then related how the money the LAPD seized was his.

He stated on the afternoon of March 21, 1990, he went to the home of one of his investors, a woman who resided at in the house in the 1300 block of S. Orange Grove, Los Angeles, an executive secretary, to consummate an investment deal. She said she dated a man who was very rich and owned pharmacies and real estate, but she did not remember his name. Also at the meeting was another investor, who turned out to be the daughter of the woman. The woman gave Wilson $300,000 in bundled currency and $58,000 from her daughter. The women then signed a contract with the preacher to build an electronic "Dr. Martin Luther King Jr. Talking Doll." Both women had the highest confidence in the preacher because they were all members of "Fisherman's Lodge."

The preacher then put the money in a dark-colored travel bag and placed it in the trunk of the car belonging to his girlfriend, the 1988 Honda Accord. At no time did the preacher ever count the money or know precisely what he had. The preacher then went over to his girlfriend's residence. They then went out to eat in her vehicle so the preacher's wife would not recognize him. Later, the girlfriend dropped the preacher off at his house. The preacher then remembered he had left the money in his girlfriend's car, but she could not be located. He later talked to her on the phone, and she said she had borrowed the car from her friend and did not know anything about the missing money. The preacher then went to bed. The preacher said he mistakenly left the money in the trunk of his car, which was loaned to the female who was stopped by police. The preacher and the investors made no effort to contact the police regarding the disappearance of their currency. The preacher's first inquiry was 19 days later after the incident. The preacher did his business dealings in cash because he said he did not trust banks. What is strange is that he only made a claim for the actual amount of currency seized by the police and not the $358,000 he supposedly received from the investors. The preacher was unable to provide documentation regarding the contract signed by him and the investors.

When I asked the preacher what the electronic doll would say, he replied, "I have a dream." I then asked what the second thing the electronic doll would say. The preacher apparently did not think I would ask that question and appeared stumped by the question. Then he replied, "Ah, ah, ah." I then asked what the third thing the doll would say, and the minister and attorney were very anxious to change the line of questioning. My partner had to hold back laughing out loud and looked at me, and we both were in disbelief. In addition, the preacher was unable to show any documentation wherein he had permission from the estate of Dr. Martin Luther King Jr. for the creation and sale of the electronic doll.

After the meeting, I then spoke on the telephone with the real pastor of the Baptist Church. The pastor emphatically stated that the preacher did not serve at his church. He said he did lead scriptures but did not preach and was not paid for his work. The pastor thought the preacher was in the toy business but did not know anything more about him.

When I got back to my office and shared the explanation with my fellow detectives, they said the first thing you need to do is contact the wife of Dr. Martin Luther King Jr. and find out if the story was on the level. I telephoned her and asked her if she had heard of the preacher and his creation of a Dr. Martin Luther King Jr. talking doll. She responded she had never heard of the preacher and that the idea of a talking doll was preposterous and blasphemy to her husband. The story got even worse. A few days later, I got a telephone call from the producer of the Phil Donohue Show, wanting to know about my investigation and that the preacher was going to go on the program and talk about the LAPD stealing his money. I told the producer if they put on this show, it would embarrass Phil Donohue no end. Later, the producer called me and said the show would not do the story. In my investigation, I learned the benefactors, the investors, got the money from the Playboy Crips street gang. During the trial of the seized money in federal court, a third attorney representing the preacher told the judge the story about the talking doll. The prosecution was prepared to have the informant and undercover officers testify about the drug deal, but it turned out not to be necessary. The judge found the defendant's story to be completely preposterous and awarded the seized money to the government.

Chapter 11

Like a Box of Chocolates, You Never Know What You're Going to Get

One of the elements of California's asset forfeiture law was that investigators should renew training on asset forfeiture every year. Classes on asset forfeiture encompassed 40 hours of accounting and bookkeeping, attendance at one of three sessions (24 hours) of training by the California District Attorneys Association state-wide, and federal training on money laundering. My experiences in asset forfeiture landed me a position as an instructor for the CDAA for over 15 years. I challenged attendees to go where no asset forfeiture investigator had gone before. As a result, I learned various investigative and money laundering techniques from many of the attendees in my classes and shared this information with future attendees.

One of the attendees was an investigator from the California Franchise Tax Board. She had an investigation that had her perplexed as to how to investigate and prosecute embezzlement by a head cashier at the University of California at San Francisco. The University was in the process of merging its financial department with Stanford University. During an audit of both institutions, an independent accounting firm discovered as much as $9 million dollars were missing from donated funds to the UCSF.

The investigation by the FTB identified a 17-year employee as the head/supervisor cashier responsible for depositing checks and cash from services such as campus parking, patient co-payments, and donations to the university, but instead pocketed most of the money. When the Vice Chancellor of UCSF found out about the results of the audit, he allegedly shared the information with the cashier. The cashier then had the records purged by having them burnt and thereby thought she had destroyed her financial trail. Through U.S. Treasury databases, the FTB investigator learned the female had made numerous deposits at banks in the greater San Francisco Bay area over the past three years.

I then suggested to the FTB investigator to obtain search warrants for each of the banks identified. Upon receiving the bank records, the FTB investigator sent them to me for analysis. I put them into a spreadsheet to illustrate each of her deposits in the accounts. I also provided the FTB with a chart showing the timing of deposits she made into several different banks on her 21-mile drive from work at UCSF to the other side of the bay to her home in Moraga. She typically would collect well over $10,000 in a shopping bag. If all the money totaled more than $10,000 in one bank account, a bank would be required to do a CTR. To avoid a CTR, on her way home in her new automobile, she would stop at a bank and deposit $3,000, then stop at another bank and deposit $3,000, and continue making stops at different banks until she had deposited all the embezzled money. The different banks would not know of her stops and, thereby, would not do any reporting of the cash deposits.

She deposited cash in this way almost daily and sometimes had other family members assist her. According to San Francisco's The Daily, she "was fired in July 1999 after she came under suspicion of pulling off one of the largest thefts in UCSF history." She was arrested for embezzling public money, grand theft, money laundering, and tax fraud. She pleaded guilty and admitted to embezzling $4.5 million to bankroll a now-defunct New Age magazine and angel-theme gallery run by her daughter's company in Lafayette, CA. The company was dedicated to the proposition that "angels are spiritual messengers dedicated to our growth and good fortune," according to The Daily article. When her daughter was questioned about the sudden wealth, she replied, "...the money came from angels."

He Did Not Come "Clean"

On February 1, 1990, Mid-Level Unit detectives received an anonymous citizen's complaint that illicit drugs were being sold at a single-family dwelling in Reseda by a male by the name of "Robert." Shortly thereafter, a confidential, reliable informant, directed by narcotics detectives, purchased an "8-ball" (a 1/8 ounce of cocaine) for $120 from a male, later identified as Robert, at the residence. Narcotics detectives tested the substance, and it tested positive. On February 7, narcotics detectives obtained a search warrant for the residence. The suspect, after waiving his constitutional rights, stated there was marijuana in the house but no money or other contraband. During the search, detectives recovered 17 grams of cocaine powder; 7.2 grams of marijuana, a triple-beam scale, and a set of weights; a rifle and a computer.

Detectives also seized for asset forfeiture as proceeds of narcotics sales, $80,978 in cash and a 1987 Chevrolet Corvette. A K-9 alerted to the presence of illicit narcotics on the money. Robert also stated, "I sell cars and sell a little white stuff on the side. I'm not going to lie; you've found all I got." Detectives also found paperwork showing he was doing business as "Impressive

Cleaning Service" and "Spectacular Effects Wholesale." He was arrested for possession of cocaine for sale. On February 8, narcotics detectives searched his bank account and seized, as proceeds, $2,352. On March 2, I obtained a search warrant for his accountant and learned the income from his businesses from 1987-1989 totaled $366,658, from which he made a $45,000 down payment on his house, purchased a 1989 Corvette, a 1987 Bombardier Jet Ski, a 1989 mini outboard boat and trailer, big-screen TV and stereo, expensive jewelry and spent $5,800 on cash purchases. No one ever saw him do any work at his business. He could not provide any customer names or references for jobs completed. He represented himself to banks as an up-and-coming entrepreneur.

Toy Box

An LAPD motorcycle officer stopped a female motorist speeding on the street in North Hollywood Division. As the officer approached the driver, he observed a large, open toy box on the backseat behind the driver. A closer look revealed bundles of currency. When the officer asked the driver about the money, she said she knew nothing about it. The officer arrested the woman and transported her and the money to the North Hollywood police station for further investigation. The officer found the box contained $400,000 in U.S. Currency. Section 11370.6(A) of the California Health and Safety Code (possessing more than $100,000 in unexplained currency) is a felony and seized for asset forfeiture. Later, an attorney representing the woman telephoned me and stated the seized money was the proceeds from selling 40 head of cattle at a ranch in Culiacan, Sinaloa, Mexico. The attorney then faxed me a copy of the sales contract. I contacted the FBI Legal Attaché in Mexico, the Cattlemen's Association, and Drug

Enforcement Administration to review the contract. All three entities found the agreement to be false.

A few months later, a detective in Northern California was in an asset forfeiture class I was teaching and approached me after class. She told me almost the same circumstances occurred in her jurisdiction wherein a woman claimed $400,000 in cash was proceeds from the sale of cattle. The exact attorney handling this contract was the same as the contract I had received earlier, except the dates were different. Later, the attorney lost his license, and the monies were forfeited.

$5.7 Million

I was sitting at my desk in asset forfeiture when I received a telephone call from an Organized Crime and Vice Division detective serving a search warrant in the Los Feliz District of Los Angeles. The detective assisted the Board of Equalization investigators in investigating an accountant, at her apartment, for Korean Organized Crime (KOC). While they conducted their search, the detective came across two suitcases filled with 57 bundles of U.S. Currency, with each bundle inside a Crown Regal velvet pouch. At closer examination, each bundle appeared to hold $100,000 in $100 bills. The accountant refused to say anything about the money. The detective was unsure if the money could be forfeited. I told him it could, and he gave me directions to the apartment. Because the money was associated with KOC, I arranged an armored escort of the funds by the SWAT (Special Weapons and Tactics) team to the bank. What was highly unusual, all the serial numbers of the $100 bills were in exact sequence totaling $5.7 million.

Two days after the seizure, I learned that a KOC courier was supposed to transport the two suitcases with the money to Seoul, South Korea, the day police seized it. Instead, the next day, the courier was shot in the face, point blank, and killed. It was puzzling because the courier, a self-defense expert, and the shooter were standing face-to-face.

During the investigation, the KOC generated millions from selling illicit drugs, gambling, prostitution, loansharking, and liquor sales from numerous nightclubs in Korea Town. The ill-gotten gains were then deposited into a money service business which converted the cash at complacent banks to $100 bills. The KOC then used the $100 bills to pay city and government officials bribes, invest in real estate, buy drugs, and further operations.

Rampart Division Corruption Scandal

In the late 1990s, a widespread scandal rocked the LAPD Rampart Division and the Department. A Narcotics Division undercover officer exposed a Rampart Division detail named Community Resources Against Street Hoodlums (CRASH), consisting of street cops, was accused of several crimes, including false reporting and arrests, robbery, planting evidence, stealing, and selling illicit drugs.

The CRASH unit consisted of a handful of police officers and a sergeant. The underlying problem was no constant supervision. As a result, they had free rein to do their work. Unfortunately, they also submitted chits for overtime that they did not work. No one ever challenged the chits, including supervisors all the way up to the commanding officer of the division.

The ringleader of the unit was an officer named Rafael, who went by "Ray," a nine-year veteran of the LAPD. A former U.S. Marine, he gained a reputation as a tough and effective officer. Unfortunately, Ray was also alleged to be a member of a notorious street gang. He later implicated 70 officers. The department investigation found 24 officers guilty of committing wrongdoings. The district attorney overturned 100 convictions because of the scandal.

The LAPD arrested Ray for stealing six pounds of cocaine from the department property room. The street value of the cocaine was $800,000. The LAPD formed a task force of specialized detectives from the Internal Affairs and Robbery Homicide Divisions to investigate Ray and the accused officers. Unfortunately, Ray's December 1998 trial ended as a mistrial. The jury had voted 8-4 in favor of acquittal.

The task force then approached me to conduct a financial analysis of the evidence collected against Ray. The task force gave me a time limit of 10 days to put together my findings.

I reviewed hundreds of documents. In my analysis, I first examined Ray and his wife's income and deposits in 1997.

Year	Income	Deposits	*Difference
1997	$105,204	$175,899	$70,695

* The difference is unexplained income.

Next, I reviewed income versus deposits in January and February 1998. I illustrated Ray and his wife's earnings on a timeline. They both worked for the LAPD and had accounts at two financial institutions. Finally, there was a total difference of $24,893 in unexplained income.

Month	Income	Deposited	Difference
Jan 1998	$ 7,193	$28,974	$21,781
Feb 1998	$ 7,293	$10,405	$ 3,112
Totals	$14,486	$39,379	$24,893

The couple had over $95,588 in unexplained deposits over 14 months. In addition, two suspicious cash deposits totaling $12,000 at a bank allegedly were structuring and money laundering.

- On January 14, Ray opened a Money Market with $6,000 cash in his child's name.

- On January 21, Ray deposited $6,000 cash into his child's Money Market account.

I put together an indictment of Ray and his wife, charging the felony crimes of money laundering and structuring transactions to avoid a Currency Transaction Report. The District Attorney and defense counsel reviewed the indictment. After that, Ray confessed to stealing cocaine and other charges and was sentenced to state prison.

Conducting Training

Becoming a subject matter expert on asset forfeiture, money laundering, and drug trafficking investigations allowed me to relate what I had learned by teaching these subjects to my peers and law enforcement officers. I taught "Asset Forfeiture," "Financial Investigative Techniques," "Money Laundering," and an "Overview of Medical Marijuana" to the California Narcotics Officers Association, Western States Information Network, annual Southwest Border Money Laundering Conference in Scottsdale,

Arizona, Arizona Department of Public Safety, Minnesota State Police, and the LAPD. However, one of my most gratifying experiences was providing instruction on behalf of the California District Attorneys Association. For over ten years, I traveled to every corner of California to present financial investigative techniques to local law enforcement officers on behalf of the CDAA. Ursula Donofrio coordinated the courses. The instructors with me were retired Judge Armando G. "Andy" Cuellar, Judge Jonathan Koresh, Asset Forfeiture experts Lee Carter, Debbie Geisser, Kevin "Bones" Maloney, Phil Urie, Pam Underwood, Ron Lillard, Dee Edgeworth, and law enforcement officers Al Salerno, Kent Shaw, and Jon Carver.

A Detective Supervisor Who Taught Ethics

In addition to the CDAA and CNOA, I taught asset forfeiture, search warrant techniques, seizing computers, and money laundering to LAPD personnel. One of the fellow supervisors I trained with was Roger. Roger worked for years in narcotics enforcement. Roger taught the complicated subject of "Ethics." He also said, "You did not want Packer investigating you. He never lets up."

Los Angeles International Airport (LAX) is the fourth busiest airport in the world and the second most active in the United States, based on the number of passengers. LAX also ranks 10th in the world and 4th in the U.S. in air cargo tonnage processed, with more than 2.4 million tons of freight and mail. Criminals see LAX as an opportunity to smuggle illicit drugs and other contraband without interference. Narcotics Division partnered with the DEA and other state and federal law enforcement agencies to create a task force at LAX to prevent drugs and bulk currency from smuggling into and out of the airport.

Most investigations went like this. For example, the LAX task force received information from a task force at Chicago O' Hare Airport about a suspected drug courier traveling from Chicago to LAX carrying contraband. Roger, a detective supervisor, and members of the task force met the flight and watched for the courier. When the courier was spotted, agents approached him and asked him to look in his carry-on luggage. The courier consented to a search, and the task force found he was carrying rolls of hundred-dollar bills. The courier denied knowing anything about the currency. The agents then seized the money for asset forfeiture and gave the courier a receipt. It was then Roger's job to count the money. To do so, he went to a side room to use a money counter. Unbeknownst to him, a new agent in the task force was nearby and saw Roger pocket some of the money. The agent was shocked and told another supervisor what he saw. Roger then came up with a total count and sealed the money in a bag placed in a safe until an asset forfeiture detective could pick it up.

One of the task force supervisors notified the commanding officer, who forwarded the information to Internal Affairs Division. Next, an IAD supervisor set up another currency seizure to verify the misconduct. The IAD then told the task force a female passenger was arriving from a Dallas flight suspected of carrying contraband in her carry-on. The task force met the female, and she consented to a search of her bag. Inside were several bundles of hundred-dollar bills. She denied knowing anything about the money. Agents then seized the money for asset forfeiture. Roger then retrieved the bag and took it to the backroom office to count it. Unbeknownst to Roger, the cash totaled $19,000. When Roger finished counting the money, he said there was a total of $16,000.

Instead of calling Roger into his lieutenant's office to confront him with the misconduct, IAD chose to arrest him as he left the office to go home at the end of his shift. Incredibly, the squad of IAD plainclothes detectives decided to make the arrest but did not know Roger's face. As the officers and Roger left for the day, the IAD detectives yelled for Roger to put his hands up. Instead, the officers and Roger reacted like they would soon be under attack and drew their weapons. Fortunately, an officer calmed the situation down to where the two sides could talk. Who knows what would have happened in the middle of the airport had there been shots fired? The IAD officers took Roger into custody without further incident.

Next, the IAD officers obtained a search warrant for Roger's home. I was called in at the last moment to assist with the search. Unfortunately, none of the IAD officers understood how to do a financial investigation and needed to figure out what to collect. Nevertheless, I found evidence showing Roger had been stealing money for an extended period. In addition, IAD officers also recovered some of the missing hundred-dollar bills seized from the female courier.

Roger was prosecuted and pleaded guilty to grand theft and other charges as a condition of his sentencing, Roger left law enforcement and served lengthy probation and paid restitution.

Illegal Cigarettes

Police officers and detectives in the field were required to contact the Asset Forfeiture Detail whenever they recovered $5,000 in cash or more.

The Rampart Field Enforcement Section narcotics officers called me and said they recovered $126,755 in cash stacked on a kitchen table in an apartment. The officers also found hundreds of cartons of illegal cigarettes throughout the apartment. The officers had earlier received information that unknown people were selling illicit drugs from the location. However, the people inside were not selling drugs. Instead, they sold smuggled cigarettes and piled the cash on the table.

Smuggled cigarettes enter the U.S. without paid domestic duties (tax evasion). Illegal cigarettes are priced much cheaper than legal cigarettes and have no health warnings. The Bureau of Alcohol, Tobacco, and Firearms investigates smuggled cigarettes.

I telephoned an agent with the BATF and discussed the officers' investigation with him. The agent then adopted the money for asset forfeiture and seized 989 cartons of illegal cigarettes. It was the first LAPD cigarette case which led to many more investigations.

"It Looked Like Over $1 Million"

The U.S. Department of State Bureau of Diplomatic Security (DSS) agents had finally located a passport fraud suspect at a mansion in the Hollywood Hills. The estate sat at the top of a narrow cul-de-sac and had an unobstructed view of the street below. As agents drove along the street, the suspect saw them. He grabbed what he could and sped off in his SUV. The agents began chasing the suspect but had trouble making U-turns to go after the suspect. Finally, an agent radioed for help. The dispatcher notified the LAPD Hollywood Division patrol watch commander, told her the DSS agents needed help, and gave them the address. An LAPD helicopter responded, as did several patrol cars. The police caught the suspect and placed him in custody. While searching his vehicle, they observed a bag on the floorboards containing excessive cash. An officer contacted the watch commander and said there were over a million dollars in the back of the truck. The watch commander then telephoned the bureau commander and said the cash was over one million. The commander then called me at Asset Forfeiture.

As I responded to the mansion, I got a frantic telephone call from a DEA agent wanting to know why I had arrested the suspect. I needed clarification. I said I was responding to a call from officers in the field who had taken the suspect into custody. The agent said she had a wiretap on the suspect. I told her to meet me at the estate.

I met with the DSS agents, the LAPD, and the DEA agent and worked out a solution. First, I obtained a search warrant for the suspect's vehicles and residence under the guise of an LAPD investigation and not identifying DSS or the DEA. I then seized whatever the agents needed for their respective investigations. The suspect had more cash and contraband hidden behind the bricks of his fireplace. The bag with the cash turned out to be only $65,000. The suspect was convicted of passport fraud and drug trafficking and is serving a lengthy prison term.

Impostor

I had just left my office to go home when I got a telephone call from the Commanding Officer of the Hollywood Division. Captain Michael Moriarty was in the middle of a jurisdictional dispute between the LAPD and DEA. Because I was a DEA Task Force Officer, he felt I could straighten the mess. Here's what I learned.

An LAPD motorcycle officer stopped a suspected female drunk driver who was a Korean national. After the woman failed a Field Sobriety Test, the officer summoned a patrol car to take her to the station for processing. While waiting for transportation, a male, Justin, a Korean national, approached the officer and flashed a DEA badge. Justin stated he was a Special Agent assigned to the Orange County District Office. He noted the female was one of his informants and asked to take custody of her. The officer noticed Justin appeared to be under the influence of alcohol and had him and the woman transported to the Hollywood station. The watch commander called the DEA Duty Agent, who sent a DEA supervisor to the station. Unfortunately, the supervisor was unsuccessful in positively identifying Justin or his informant. The situation between the LAPD and DEA lasted all day until the commanding officer called me.

Based on the events, I wrote and served a search warrant for Justin, the female's vehicles, and Justin's residence in Glendale. The trunk of Justin's vehicle contained an assortment of federal and state law enforcement badges and identification cards. In addition, a trove of federal and state police gear, badges, weapons, body armor, raid shirts and jackets, and printing equipment to make identification cards was in his residence. Justin admitted that he sold these items to street gangs. As a result, for impersonating a federal agent, Justin was sentenced to prison.

Go Where No Asset Forfeiture Detective Has Gone Before!

Narcotics detectives arrested a husband and wife for dealing illicit drugs in Sylmar, CA. The wife had four California Identification Cards and one Washington State Identification Card. The

Washington card listed an address in Yakima. In addition, detectives seized a large amount of cash.

I was assigned the asset forfeiture investigation. First, I researched the suspect's home in Sylmar and Yakima addresses and wrote a search warrant for both locations. At the Sylmar house, it was empty of furniture and belongings. I then flew up to Yakima, and the Yakima Police Department assisted me with writing a Washington search warrant and serving it. The drug dealer was in disbelief that an LAPD detective had discovered his residence. Besides seizing a new pickup truck in the driveway, I took more cash inside the house and illicit drugs. I also found money in a Yakima bank account.

Presidential Security Detail

Prior to the Democratic National Convention at Staples Center, August 14-17, 2000, I was selected along with other Narcotics Division supervisors to team with U.S. Secret Service agents from various parts of the country to provide protective responsibilities throughout the convention. After several days of training, I was assigned to a team of Secret Service agents from Tennessee and Kentucky to guard the First Lady, Hillary Clinton, and her daughter Chelsea. I was impressed with the dedication and professionalism of the Secret Service agents. After my first full day with the team, I had to put my feet in a tub full of ice at the end of the day. Agents are sometimes on their feet 18 hours a day or longer.

Chapter 12

God Was Watching Over Me

On June 28, 1990, at 11:00 am, I nearly lost my life. I drove my unmarked police vehicle to an FBI meeting with the Conquest task force in the San Fernando Valley. My lieutenant was following me. As traffic began to slow on the northbound 101 freeway near Vineland Avenue, a truck suddenly jack-knifed in front of me. I braked and swerved toward the center divider to avoid a collision. Unfortunately, as my front tire hit the center divider, my vehicle started to roll, flipped over several times, and slid across all four lanes to a stop on the shoulder. The roof caved in down to the steering wheel.

A week earlier, I watched a TV program about vehicle rollovers, and it was suggested the driver turn and grab the passenger seat and lay low to avoid injury. It worked. I had to crawl through the vehicle and out the rear. People who saw the car could not believe the driver had survived. As I tried to stand up, my back would not allow me to stand upright. My lieutenant told me to sit down and called an ambulance. The paramedics put me on a stretcher and went to St. Joseph Hospital in Burbank. Upon arrival, another ambulance arrived with a male my age having a heart attack. The doctors took him first and wheeled me into a darkened area. My lieutenant came moments later and thought the heart attack patient was me and to notify my wife.

A short time later, one of the captains from the Narcotics Division arrived at the hospital. She stood near the bay with the heart attack victim and watched as the doctors worked on him feverously. My lieutenant could not locate my wife and called one of my friends. Then, the heart attack patient died. I was getting restless, and my left foot itched, but I could not scratch it and yelled for somebody to help me. My captain, who was in tears, heard me and came into the area where I was. She then started yelling to the doctors that I was alive. The confused doctors ran to my room, cleared up the mistake, and began to treat me. Fortunately, I had no fractures or serious injuries. They did find I had numerous pulled muscles in my back and held me overnight for observation. The hospital ward was under construction, so they put me in the maternity ward for the night. The nurse in charge was very mean to me. Afterward, I found out she had recently divorced a cop. After ten days of healing, I went back to work.

Kinneloa Mesa Fire Rescue

On October 27, 1993, my close friend, George Taylorson, telephoned me at 4:30 am and asked me if I could help him move his livestock from his property because of a fire spreading through a canyon near his house. George and his wife Sharry resided on a ranch property on Kinneloa Mesa, above Altadena. I looked out my second-floor window in Arcadia (just over four miles from Kinneloa Mesa) and could see a massive orange glow against the hillsides to the north. I dressed so fast that I put on two different colored socks and shoes. I had no time to lose. I then drove my van up to George's house. I turned on the garden hose, but there was no water pressure. I also felt a warm air draft going uphill as I helped George move his horses from the stable to the road. He and Sharry then led them down the hill to a safe area with other residents and their livestock. It looked like animals heading for Noah's Ark. I noticed that few people were awake in the neighborhood, so I started banging on doors to wake people up. I awoke the residents at one house as the fire was ablaze in their backyard, and they were unaware of it. Next, I canvassed every street on the mesa until everyone knew of the imminent disaster. Unfortunately, no firefighters were in the area yet.

Returning to George's house, his next-door neighbor's house exploded into flames. I went into George's house, removed what I thought were sentimental objects, boxes, saddles, guns, all the items in their master bathroom drawers, medicine chest, and clothing, and loaded them into my van. I knew Sharry was a teacher, so I grabbed notebooks I saw on her desk and put them in my van. Later, the notebooks itemized all their possessions, and a box contained thousands of dollars in cash. As the smoke began to permeate the house, the last thing I took off a wall made a big hole. I thought I would be in trouble with George. As I got to my car, George's house exploded into flames. After directing firefighters, I drove to George's brother's house in Pasadena and unloaded my van in his garage. Later, when I met with George and Sharry, I told them I grabbed some things from their house and put them in his brother's garage. These items were the only possessions saved from the house. Interviewed on KNBC Channel 4 about my actions, L.A. Times sportswriter Elliott Teaford also reported, "Announcer Packer lends a hand during the fire and came to the rescue of several homeowners when fire swept into an Altadena neighborhood." As a result, the LAPD awarded me the Police Star medal for bravery.

Procrastination Saved the Day

On February 28, 1997, during the Mule Train task force, I worked at an off-site office and prepared to pick up evidence at a Bank of America branch on Laurel Canyon Blvd and Kittridge Street in North Hollywood. At approximately 8:30 am, I was about to leave when I got an urgent telephone call from fellow detective Eric "Tater" Lundquist, asking, "Weren't you supposed to be picking up evidence at the Bank of America?" I said I was heading that way, and Tater said to turn on the police radio. So, I did and heard frantic officers yelling about a shootout at the bank. Known later as the "North Hollywood Shootout," two heavily armed and armored bank robbers held up the Bank of America for over 44 minutes, confronted police, and fired thousands of rounds of ammunition. I would have been at the center of the firefight.

Chapter 13

Organized Crime Drug Enforcement Task Forces

From 1990 through 2008, while a detective in the LAPD Asset Forfeiture Detail, I was a deputized Task Force Officer (TFO) with six different Organized Crime Drug Enforcement Task Forces (OCDETF) with the FBI, IRS, and DEA in Los Angeles and Wichita, Kansas. An OCDETF is an independent component of the U.S. Department of Justice. Its purpose is to combat transnational organized crime and reduce the availability of illicit narcotics by using a prosecutor-led, multi-agency approach to enforcement.

Conquest OCDETF

On May 3, 1990, I accompanied Asset Forfeiture Investigative Unit Detective Supervisor Don Brown to a spacious house in Walnut, California, where he assigned me to the asset forfeiture investigation. There, I learned from Major Narcotics detectives that they served a search warrant on a 19-year-old heroin trafficker Jose Trinidad Lopez-Beltran, known as "Mario." Before his arrest, Mario told undercover detectives he could provide kilogram quantities of heroin. During surveillance of Mario, detectives observed him drop off a package containing 311 grams of heroin in a bush next to a fast-food restaurant in Montclair, CA. Then he retrieved another box containing $122,457. Mario's 18-year-old wife, Maria Elena Mendoza, and two others were observed driving south on Highway 15 enroute near the Salton Sea and stopped by police. After the arrest, detectives obtained a search warrant for Mario's house in Walnut. In addition to a total of $189,290 in cash, five expensive automobiles and numerous items of personal property for asset forfeiture. While searching the residence, I observed a huge oil painting of the couple with 65 wedding attendants on one of the walls in the living room. On another wall was a tall portrait of Mario and his bride. I later learned the wedding had taken place at St. Vincent de Paul Roman Catholic Church in Los Angeles and the wedding reception at the Los Angeles Convention Center.

The house's interior was like a palace with Italian marble, expensive furnishings, and numerous stereo and television equipment. I also found two thick wedding albums, which also were seized to identify wedding attendees. Later, federal agents reviewed the album and identified several drug traffickers. Two of the traffickers were in a drug trafficking organization that later became the Sinaloa Cartel in Mexico. Another person in the album was identified as the uncle of Mario's wife, serving a lengthy prison sentence at Terminal Island Federal Penitentiary for trafficking 500 kilograms of cocaine.

After several weeks, a financial investigation revealed how Mario and his wife acquired the house and other properties through fraud. The analysis also identified 69-year-old Henry Cleveland, who owned realty offices in Montebello and Fontana, CA. Henry sold the house to Mario and his wife using fictitious names. Research revealed Henry was involved in the purchase and sale of 1,143 properties in the same manner as Mario and his wife. In addition, Henry was the lynchpin of a significant money laundering scheme involving Mexican and Colombian drug trafficking organizations.

The money laundering scheme involved Henry's brothers, a close friend, and Paul, a fired LAPD officer. Paul was a loan underwriter at a bank, one brother worked at an escrow company, one at a title company, and his friend handled home and auto insurance matters.

The process went like this: Henry's realty office identified a home for purchase. The drug trafficking organizations provided Henry cartons and boxes filled with bulk currency. Henry then had several individuals deposit the cash at one of four banks. The bank tellers on Henry's payroll would then deposit the cash, and either fail to report the money with the IRS reporting standards or deposit the cash in multiple bank accounts. The branch also allowed persons to open multiple safe deposit box accounts, filling them with illicit drugs such as cocaine, unreported currency, jewelry, and firearms. One trafficker, named "Miguel," pictured in one of Mario's wedding albums, used an alias of Juan Beltran to open 88 safe deposit boxes at one branch of a bank. Miguel owned a local fish restaurant and provided shrimp and crab to bank employees on Fridays. I showed the teller a picture of Miguel. She identified him as Juan.

Henry then gave the underwriter a potential buyer with a fictitious name(s) or actual individual(s), fictitious Social Security Numbers, fictitious employment, and fictitious bank accounts. In the case of Mario and his wife, their fictitious names were "Martin and Julia Lopez." The Uniformed Residential Loan Application, completed by the loan underwriter, listed their fictitious employment with substantial salaries, fake bank accounts, and false assets and liabilities. The lender noted, "Borrowers have no established credit, but income is good, jobs are stable, plenty of net worth to show they purchase with cash down payment is coming from the sale of a residence."

For example, the loan underwriter completed the Uniform Residential Loan Application for a female trafficker named Dora. Her employment was "E&G Lighting, 10141 Rush Street, South El Monte, CA, as a saleswoman selling lamps, earning $6,800 per month and had worked there for three years." The business turned out to be a rented space with a telephone answered by a woman posing as the fictitious manager of E&G Lighting. When a bank or loan officer telephoned the business, the person answering would say the verified employee worked at the firm and earned a substantial income. Over 380 of the 1,143 loan applications reviewed by the task force used E&G Lighting as their place of employment. Dora also listed a balance of $210,000 in her savings account at the bank.

Later in the investigation, Dora's husband, Felix Cornejo Sosa, a Mexican drug lord, owned several homes purchased through Henry in Colton, Hacienda Heights, Downey, Fresno, and Chula Vista that were in the process of being seized by the task force. Felix telephoned me from Mexico and sought to negotiate a deal to halt the proceedings. He invited me to meet him in Guadalajara. Unfortunately, I did not make the trip. Later, Felix was assassinated in Culiacan.

During a search of the bank's safe deposit boxes, a receipt showed Miguel purchased 45 acres of land in the proposed model city of California City, near Mojave. The town had paved streets and street signs with the names of makes of automobiles. The developers even put in fake utility hole covers. The land broker had tricked Miguel. The acreage and other parcels turned out to be in the flight path of an air force base runway. The Los Angeles

District Attorney's Office prosecuted the land broker for bilking hundreds of thousands of dollars from innocent Hispanics and Miguel. I also observed some unique lamps in Miguel's house that were purchased in Downey for his residence. I contacted the furniture store where the lights were purchased and learned of members of his trafficking organization who also bought the same lamps as he had, with addresses of where each lamp was delivered. This information gave us new suspects to target.

During interviews with bank employees, they stated that boxes of cash were brought into the bank by people whose appearances did not reflect having that kind of money. The bank teller did not complete any CTRs. Investigators found one of the accounts belonged to two brothers who owned two used car dealerships in Bell, California. One of the brothers was a convicted drug trafficker. Agents seized $462,094 from their accounts.

Figure 37: After announcing a search warrant for a residence, the arrestee was in possession of this AR-15. He said my voice sounded like the announcer at Dodger Stadium.

Because of the magnitude of the investigation, we applied for an OCDETF led by agents from the Federal Bureau of Investigation. In those days, for a task force to be approved, Detective Supervisor Hugh Wilton and I had to travel to Washington, D.C., to present the case to an OCDETF Committee with the Office of the Attorney General. We named the task force "Condor" and envisioned catching drug traffickers in our talons. But the FBI renamed the task force "Conquest." Finally, it was approved and given $1 million for operating expenses and another $1 million to be laundered. Led by Lieutenant Harold "Skip" Tucker, Detective III Bob Baker, and Detective II Hugh Wilton, and several detectives and myself from AFIU, the task force consisted of an LAPD surveillance crew led by Detective II Tom Chambers and Special

Agents James Livingston and Mary Rook from the FBI, U.S. Customs Service, Immigration and Naturalization Service (now known as Homeland Security) Special Agent Thomas O'Brien, and Special Agents Sadie Towler and Rich Kakita from the Internal Revenue Service. In addition, Assistant U.S. Attorneys Karen J. Immergut, Eric Honig, and Rob B. Villeza prosecuted task force targets.

In those days, an OCDETF operated from a neutral city for the investigation, and so we chose Pasadena. The sign over our office door said that we were an earthquake retrofitting company. I will never forget the look on the property manager's face when he mistakenly opened our office door and observed some of our undercover surveillance squad members with long hair and beards.

The task force identified a scheme by Used Car Dealerships to transport illicit drugs. Reminiscent of Clint Eastwood's movie "The Mule," cars would arrive at a dealership and pull into the mechanics' bay. Usually, kilograms of cocaine were loaded into the trunk. Suspects then drove the drugs to distributors throughout California and the U.S. If police wanted to seize a vehicle for asset forfeiture, the legal owner (Used Car Dealership) would claim more than $5,000 or more was owed on the car and provide fictitious vehicle contracts. Thereby the vehicle was returned to the dealership and sold off. The task force took aerial photos of the dealership lots for several months showing the dealer sold no cars off the lots. Yet, they would send copies of upwards of 30 sales to the Department of Motor Vehicles with fictitious information to make it appear the businesses were selling 30 vehicles monthly. Department of Motor Vehicles inspectors assisted me in obtaining photocopies of the sales receipts, and I shared them with a special agent with U.S. Customs at the San Ysidro border crossing. Nine out of ten vehicles identified were seized by U.S. Border Patrol at San Ysidro and Otay Mesa border crossings with illicit drugs. One of the vehicles that somehow got past border checkpoints was stopped by sheriff's deputies in Kings County, CA, with several kilograms of cocaine in the trunk. The deputies sought to seize the vehicle for forfeiture but were frustrated. Again, the dealership owed an excessive amount on the car, so the vehicle was returned to the dealership.

In 1992, a national database helped the task force identify 221 vehicles sold by two used car dealerships in Bell, California, with drugs that had been stopped throughout the U.S. by police. Frustratingly, in each scenario, police had to return the vehicles to the dealerships.

During the investigation, the task force arranged to have an undercover officer (referred to as a "UC") pose as a Colombian drug trafficker to get to know Henry. The UC called Henry to set up an introductory meeting at a local restaurant. The UC plan was for him to eventually launder money through Henry's operation and learn about his process. The UC finally obtained a lunch meeting with Henry. While talking, the UC recognized a man entering the restaurant as an active LAPD detective, later identified as Bob, headed toward their table. Bob was deflected momentarily by a waiter (another UC). Fearing the detective might recognize the UC, the UC immediately excused himself to the restroom. The UC then exited the bathroom through a window and left the location. This almost disastrous incident caused the task force to adopt strategies to avoid detection in future operations. Later, the task force learned Bob worked in plainclothes for the Organized Crime and Vice Division and had accessed a narcotics database searching for officers investigating Henry and other related traffickers. In one instance, the surveillance team followed one of the traffickers to a telephone booth. Shortly after a call from Bob, the trafficker looked around to detect police, nervously got into his car, and drove to Los Angeles International Airport. He then boarded a jet and flew one way to Mexico, never to be seen again. Because it might have been a coincidence, the task force took no chances, and it was a year before we could re-introduce a UC to Henry.

The task force received information on a potential female target at an apartment in Glendale, CA, and set up surveillance. A male left the location, walked to an adjacent parking lot, got into a vehicle, and drove away. One of the detectives telephoned me at the off-site office with the vehicle's plate. Moments after I had obtained information from the Department of Motor Vehicles on the license plate, I got a telephone call from a male, identifying himself as a U.S. Customs supervisor, and wanted to know why I sought information on his vehicle. Intentionally, I asked the supervisor to read out his license plate to me. He did, and I responded with a slightly different license plate than his. I told him I was sorry we got the plate mixed up with his. He said not to let that happen again and abruptly hung up. I then called the surveillance crew and told them about the call. The male that exited the apartment was the supervisor.

The task force learned that Mario was allegedly the sponsor of a Mexican professional boxer and world champion. In 1990, during one of the boxer's fights in Las Vegas, the task force conducted surveillance of the audience during the fight and observed the same LAPD detective, the U.S. Customs supervisor, and an active INS special agent, sitting with Henry and other drug traffickers near the ring. Later in the investigation, Bob and the two government agents were on Henry's payroll. Bob was the equivalent of a mafia consigliere for a Mexican drug lord, Victor Parra-Portillo, who was assassinated in Culiacan, Mexico, in 1998. These events again caused the task force to rethink undercover and field operations.

Later, we learned Henry always wanted to fly an airplane, but poor eyesight prevented him from doing so. The task force then came up with the idea to get closer to him. Our UC, continuing to pose as a Colombian cocaine trafficker, invited Henry to Miami to show him the high life at his home near Miami and go boating on one of his cigar boats. Cigar boats are known as go-fast boats, used to transport illicit drugs. But first, the UC bridged the subject to Henry of his dream of flying and arranged a particular flight aboard a jet trainer for Henry in the Mojave Desert. A pilot with the same complexion and color as the UC flew Henry at Mach speeds and performed barrel rolls and other frightening maneuvers that thoroughly thrilled Henry. Henry then jumped at the chance to meet the UC in Miami. Soon after that, Henry flew to Miami. The UC took Henry to see a wet-tee-shirt contest. Then, he drove Henry through the canals around Miami in a cigar boat at high speeds under low bridges, disregarding warning signs and the U.S. Coast Guard. Henry was again thrilled and believed the UC was a significant drug dealer. Then, in 1992, Hurricane Andrew tore through Homeward, Florida, causing $25 billion in damages. One home was ripped from its foundation, exposing kilograms of cocaine. We learned later that the Bob verified the UC's story about the cocaine and damage to the house. The UC complained to Henry that he owned the home, was tired of all the hurricanes, and wanted to buy property in Southern California. Henry took the bait and the UC's drug money and assisted him in illegally purchasing two single-family homes in Southern California.

Surveillance and wiretaps helped the task force identify Mexican and Colombian drug traffickers associated with Henry's operations. Investigations of these individuals led to their arrest and the seizure of thousands of pounds of heroin, cocaine, methamphetamine, and other illicit drugs from the traffickers. In addition, agents seized millions in cash for forfeiture.

In August 1994, as the task force neared the end of the investigation, 88 boxes of evidence containing over 250,000 documents were shipped to the National Drug Intelligence Center in Johnstown, Pennsylvania. INS Special Agent Thomas O'Brien and I then traveled to NDIC. Over the next five days, we assisted 48 DOMEX (Document and Media Exploitation) analysts in examining and interpreting the evidence in the boxes. Finally, the analysts completed their analysis and organized the documents and evidence into 13 notebooks. The notebooks identified 10 main targets of the investigation and the evidence connected to each of them. We then gave the notebooks to the U.S. Attorneys handling the prosecution.

At the end of the investigation, Henry was arrested and charged with conspiracy, money laundering, and tax evasion. Henry agreed to plead guilty and cooperated with the task force. In 1989, Henry's operation laundered $46.8 million from illicit drug sales in purchasing real estate. He identified homes and businesses in San Diego, Chula Vista, and numerous cities in Southern California used as "stash houses" to store illicit drugs and weapons or temporary lodging for human traffickers. The investigation also identified trafficking routes from Mexico to California. In addition, a corrupt former and active LAPD officer, a U.S. Customs supervisor, and an INS agent were indicted and convicted of numerous state and federal charges and sentenced to prison.

The investigation was closed in 1994. Before this task force, 19 different state and federal law enforcement agencies had targeted Henry but were unsuccessful.

The task force received numerous accolades from the U.S. Attorney General. Chief of Police Willie Williams presented me and the task force with the LAPD Meritorious Unit Citation.

Los Angeles Joint Drug Intelligence Group

Following the Conquest Task Force, Narcotics Division loaned me to the Los Angeles Joint Drug Intelligence Group in Norwalk, California, for six months. The LAJDIG housed representatives from numerous federal, state, and local law enforcement agencies and the branches of the military and the California National Guard involved in investigating drug trafficking and money laundering. The LAJDIG provided analytical databases for researching and identifying targets and their criminal organizations. A long-time friend of mine, LAPD Detective Donald Barfield, was assigned to the LAJDIG and served as a valuable resource.

Two investigations I started at the LAJDIG were from the LAPD. One involved a significant methamphetamine trafficking organization by the Clandestine Lab Squad. First, detectives identified everyone involved, where lab equipment and chemicals had been purchased or delivered, and possible clandestine lab sites in Southern and Central California. Then, using numerous government databases and media tools, such as DOMEX (Document and Media Exploitation), analysts analyzed hundreds of receipts and other documents entered into a highly sophisticated search database. Finally, the research produced evidence of the hierarchy and leaders of the organization so the detectives could further their investigation. The LAJDIG also produced a wall-sized chart showing the relationship between people, places, vehicles, and probable lab sites, which was very helpful to the lab squad and eventual prosecution.

The second investigation came from Narcotics Division's Field Enforcement Section detectives in Van Nuys, CA. They called their operation "Mule Train," after the twenty-mule train that hauled millions of pounds of Borax in Death Valley, CA. Instead, their Mule Train sought to seize "one gram at a time" of illicit drugs which would help curtail the drug trade.

The six FES detectives of Mule Train identified two Mexican DTOs (drug trafficking organizations) conducting criminal activities in the San Fernando Valley. One, the Sinaloa Cowboys (later to become the Sinaloa Cartel), operated on the east side of the 405 freeway and included North Hollywood, Van Nuys, and Foothill Divisions. The second DTO, from the Mexican state of Nayarit (Guadalajara Cartel), sold illicit drugs on the west side of the 405 and included West Valley and Devonshire Divisions. The highway was a demilitarized zone allowing free passage of both DTOs. The Sinaloa Cowboys were violent and always carried firearms and had miniature lariats or saddles hanging from their rearview mirror and a statue of Jesus Malverde on the dashboard. Malverde, a 'Robin Hood' kind of bandit, was hanged in 1909 in Culiacan, in the Mexican state of Sinaloa. However, drug dealers revered him as the "Narco-Saint," believing he would bring the Cowboys good luck. The Cowboys created shrines in their residences and wore clothing and jewelry with likenesses of Malverde.

The Mule Train investigation was my last LAJDIG assignment but not the end of the case by a longshot.

Mule Train OCDETF

Then, there were five LAPD divisions in the San Fernando Valley, North Hollywood, Van Nuys, West Valley, Devonshire, and Foothill. Each division had a Field Enforcement Section squad of 6-10 personnel dedicated entirely to narcotics enforcement. I polled each FES group about what drug dealers do with the money they make from illicit drug sales. They opined that drug dealers converted bulk drug money to money orders at Casa de Cambios or Money Service Businesses in the San Fernando Valley. There were over 50 MSBs spread throughout the San Fernando Valley. Drug dealers chose to send money orders back to their distributors in Mexico. This method of money laundering was much better and safer than transporting bulk currency to Mexico. Money orders had no scent avoiding detection at the border. In addition, because money orders represented U.S. Currency, they could be resold in Mexico and Central America for higher than their value.

One successful operation, Mule Train, targeting drug traffickers in the San Fernando Valley, was from Van Nuys Division FES. They also identified an MSB conspiring with drug dealers named Supermail International, Inc. in Reseda, CA.

Supermail International Inc. was headquartered in Sacramento and had branches throughout California. The California Department of Banking licensed MSBs. The Department had just nine inspectors who regulated the over 9,000 MSBs throughout the state. A Spanish-speaking detective and I, posing as banking inspectors, visited 25 MSBs, selected at random, and included the Supermail branch in Reseda. All of them were aware of MSB regulations, including handling and reporting large amounts of currency and the crime of money laundering. An MSB, like a bank, is a financial institution regulated by the U.S. Department of the Treasury and the Bank Secrecy Act. We were amazed at customers bringing boxes of cash to MSBs to convert to money orders. In one MSB in Northridge, there were ten electronic money counters in the rear of the business to handle large amounts of U.S. Currency. At the Supermail branch in Reseda, customers wanting to convert cash to money orders stretched around the block. This business was allegedly laundering millions in drug cash.

I brought this information to the attention of the FBI agents, and they agreed to form an OCDETF with the same name, "Mule Train." In addition to the six detectives from FES, 11 detectives were part of the OCDETF from the Narcotics Division Asset Forfeiture Detail. The neutral off-site location was an office located in Sylmar in the north San Fernando Valley. Once, a team of surveillance agents from a federal law enforcement agency thought our location was where drug dealers hung out.

In the scenario we set up, an undercover detective (UC) posed as a drug trafficker and told the manager of the Supermail business that he had lots of drug dollars to convert to money orders. Initially, the UC converted $3,000 in various denominations to $500 money orders. The next day, UC converted $5,000 to $500 money orders. We increased the amount of cash converted to $11,000 to see if the manager reported suspicious money transactions. Cash over $10,000 requires the completion of a Currency Transaction Report (CTR) filed with the Internal Revenue Service. The manager or the corporate office did not report the transactions. Failure to report a transaction is subject to a $250,000 fine per occurrence. Instead, the manager waited until the end of a business day and then said the real currency received for the day, which is against the law. The UC then brought $100,000 in $20 bills to be converted. To the UC's surprise, the manager took some of the money across the street to another different MSB to convert the cash to money orders. The UC expressed concern with the manager's actions and asked to speak to his superior, who in turn introduced the UC to a district manager. The manager also provided the UC with an individual who could transport large amounts of money orders to a bank in Mexico. The Mexican bank then arranged to convert the money orders to pesos and wire the payment to UC's international bank account. This action completed the money laundering cycle. The only loss was the laundering fees paid to the manager, the transporter, and the Mexican bank.

The UC then spoke to the regional sales manager and told him he would be converting millions to money orders. The regional sales manager then connected the UC with the senior vice president, chief executive officer, and president of the corporation in Sacramento. The UC then invited them to come aboard his yacht (an undercover yacht) to discuss further operations. The trio then flew to Los Angeles and boarded the vessel. They were treated to various food and beverages and videotaped by cameras aboard the yacht. The trio then bragged about how they could launder money through other means, including their stock portfolio. The UC then gave the trio an orange bag containing $200,000 in $20 bills as seed money.

The UC then converted thousands more cash to money orders at various branches of Supermail in Rosemead and downtown Los Angeles. But again, Supermail employees did not report any of these transactions to the IRS.

At the end of the operation, agents served search warrants and seizure orders at branches of Supermail and the corporate officer's homes.

According to the U.S. Attorney's Office press release, a 67-count federal indictment involving ten defendants charged the corporate officers with a conspiracy to launder approximately $828,500 in cash received from an undercover government agent posing as a major drug trafficker. The defendants, who faced maximum sentences of 20 years in prison, also agreed to forfeit any cash and assets received during the conspiracy.

During the overall investigation, I prepared and served 80 search warrants which resulted in the recovery of 219 guns, 456 kilograms of cocaine, ten pounds of heroin, 164 pounds of methamphetamine, 1,666 pounds of marijuana, and the seizure of $2.4 million in cash. In addition, 370 suspects were arrested on felony charges. For our efforts, the LAPD awarded the 28 members of the task force a Police Meritorious Unit Citation.

Jamaican Express West OCDETF

On October 14, 2002, Los Angeles County Sheriff's Department Lennox deputies stopped a lone motorist in a 2002 Cadillac Escalade for a traffic violation. The violator, identified as Clive, a Jamaican national, did not have a driver's license. Deputies recovered a loaded 9MM semi-automatic pistol from his waistband, a brick of marijuana under the seat, and $7,984 in cash.

Deputies charged Clive with Sections 11359 and 11360 of the California Health and Safety Code (possession/transportation of marijuana). The vehicle, owned by a female, later identified as his wife, was impounded.

On December 10, 2002, during a refueling stop at Salina Airport, Kansas, DEA Wichita agents intercepted a flight from Van Nuys Airport to Cleveland, Ohio, carrying 155 kilograms of cocaine inside six suitcases. Agents arrested one suspect named Austin, a Jamaican national.

In mid-December 2002, Dean, a Jamaican national and procurer of vehicles for a Jamaican posse (drug trafficking organization) based in Los Angeles, and his girlfriend, Cherise, also a Jamaican national, argued about their cars. Cherise drove a rundown Ford Mustang. Dean drove an expensive Cadillac Escalade, and she wanted one. Dean thought he remembered one Escalade that was available but needed help remembering where it was. So, he dialed the emergency service telephone number for the vehicle and asked if the service could locate the car. Unfortunately, the service could only find the vehicle if it had been stolen or involved in a major traffic accident. Dean then reported the vehicle stolen at the LAPD Wilshire Police Station.

On December 23, 2002, Troy, a Jamaican national residing in Chatsworth and the owner of a record company in North Hollywood, and Ondreya, a stripper from Cleveland, boarded a Lear Jet at Van Nuys Airport for a chartered flight to Cleveland. They carried with them 225 kilograms of marijuana concealed in their luggage. During a regular refueling stop in Salina, Kansas, a DEA task force based in Wichita detected illicit drugs in luggage and arrested the pair. The subjects were evasive in answering the agents' questions and did not provide any information about where they were going. Troy chartered the flight from a company based at Van Nuys Airport.

On the same day, at approximately 10:30 pm, Brian and Sean, Jamaican nationals residing in the greater Los Angeles area, flew to Detroit and arrived at 5:50 am on December 23, 2002. They boarded a commuter flight and arrived in Cleveland at 9:45 am. They paid $1,928 in cash for the tickets. They intended to meet Troy's flight, but when they learned police had intercepted him, they flew back to Los Angeles.

On December 24, 2002, at approximately 1:00 am, Clive boarded a Lear Jet with Brian and Sean at Van Nuys Airport and flew to Richmond Point Airport, Ohio. A shuttle then drove them one way to a rock house in Cleveland. The driver observed Clive carrying a duffel bag into the location. Later that day, Clive, Brian, and Sean boarded the same jet at Richmond Point Airport, with one large suitcase, for the return flight to Van Nuys Airport, arriving at 8:55 pm on December 24. The flight was paid for by a record company owned by Troy and a record company owned by Clive.

While the jet was inbound to Van Nuys Airport, LAPD Van Nuys Division patrol officers received a radio call to go to Van Nuys Airport and conduct a recovered vehicle investigation (a recovered vehicle is usually a stolen vehicle). Airport personnel advised the patrol officers that a vehicle tracking system notified them of a stolen 2002 Cadillac Escalade, 4-door black that was located behind the executive jet port. Officers checked the vehicle and found it was parked next to another 2002 Cadillac Escalade, 4-door, black. An officer then contacted the victim. Dean answered and asked the officer where the car was. The officer stated it was at Van Nuys Airport. Dean then remembered who possessed it and told the officer he wanted to "un-report" it stolen. Dean told officers that his wife, Cherise, was Christmas shopping and had left the keys in the vehicle and left it unattended. Officers asked both Dean and Cherise if they knew Clive. They both replied they did not know him. A few minutes later, Cherise telephoned the airport and stated she just wanted to get the vehicle back and was not interested in prosecuting Clive. Officers explained the nature of the crime and that making a false police report was a crime. Cherise called back and stated that the vehicle had been taken in a business dispute but would not discuss to whom the conflict was. Later, she said she did not want her husband to find out who had the car. The police then directed Dean and Cherise to come to the airport.

An airport employee then told police the occupants of the stolen vehicle and the other Cadillac Escalade would be arriving aboard a chartered jet shortly. The airport employee described the occupants as three male Jamaican nationals with no luggage. One of the men, Clive, gave him the keys to the stolen Escalade.

At approximately 8:55 pm, the jet arrived at the terminal. Clive, Brian, and Sean exited the aircraft with one large suitcase on rollers. Clive pulled the suitcase into the terminal. Brian and Sean stayed back and took positions behind obstacles. Unbeknownst to them, other police officers on the tarmac took Brian and Sean into custody without further incident. Officers then discovered the trio each had loaded semi-automatic pistols in their waistbands with armor-penetrating ammunition. Clive said the suitcase was his. The three men made no further comments regarding the flight. Officers examined the suitcase and found it contained an excessive amount of U.S. currency bundled with rubber bands inside shopping bags and shoe boxes. The money was later counted and found to be $852,405 in cash. The money was seized under asset forfeiture as proceeds of drug trafficking.

In researching law enforcement and government databases, we determined Clive, Troy, and Brian were brothers. In addition, several other family members were implicated in trafficking cocaine and marijuana and allegedly laundering millions of dollars. Based on this information, an OCDETF was formed with the LAPD and DEA entitled "Jamaican Express West." The task force targeted the Jamaican drug trafficking organization (DTO) in Los Angeles that transported cocaine and marijuana via private chartered jets to Cleveland, New York City, and Philadelphia. In addition, the targets laundered over $8 million from drug sales through investments and purchasing houses in Southern California. The DEA also uncovered a Jamaican national operating a flight service that arranged drug and bulk currency flights.

During the next two years, the task force monitored drug and bulk currency flights to see where illicit drugs went and how they laundered drug proceeds. When drugs reached a destination, the task force provided information to local police to affect an arrest and seizure. For example, the task force learned bulk currency from selling illicit drugs and was transported to Los Angeles. Female members of the DTO took the money and either structured deposits into bank accounts at various banks or converted millions in cash into money orders at 7-11 stores in Diamond Bar and Fountain Valley. In addition, the money orders were either deposited into an escrow account or numerous bank accounts, or spent on purchasing firearms, vehicles (Humvee and Escalades), food, personal items, furniture, motion picture film ventures, recording businesses, and even swimming pools, decks, and grottos.

In one motion picture, a casting director reported two men (one was Brian) would show up at a film sight carrying automatic weapons and suitcases filled with cash to meet payroll (all the movie personnel were paid in cash).

Clive owned a recording studio in Los Angeles as a front for doing business to cover his drug trade. Clive staged photographs of Rap artists at various high rises around Los Angeles. He then made CDs containing his extensive music repertoire and distributed them to people he did business with to make his company look prosperous.

Troy owned a recording studio in North Hollywood and lived in a spacious mansion atop a hill in Chatsworth. His gold-inlaid furniture was audacious. Troy and Clive had in common swimming pools with caves and grottos built by the same pool company.

Faith, Clive's sister, had several aliases and acted as the DTO's real estate salesperson. She used dead people as buyers of real estate. Faith had a Notary who would forge signatures and fingerprints with fake driver's licenses. She invested drug dollars in the purchase of over 30 large homes throughout Southern California.

A federal grand jury in Topeka, Kansas, indicted the nine targets of the DTO. The task force sought to arrest everyone in early November 2003. However, a slipup by the U.S. Attorney's Office (AUSA) in Topeka, a clerk sent an email to one of the defense attorneys. The email contained the names of the targets and the takedown date. The AUSA immediately contacted me after the email went out, and we coordinated an emergency takedown with available personnel. By the afternoon, the task force arrested six of the nine targets, some at airports. One escaped to Jamaica.

While incarcerated before their trials, the targets telephoned family members. When a target picked up the receiver, a voice told the caller the conversation was being recorded. Despite this warning, the target-directed family members to go to a particular bank and withdraw money from accounts they kept secret. Over one year, the task force seized several million dollars after listening to the conversations.

The U.S. Marshal's Service caught Faith and Sean several years later.

The targets were prosecuted and are serving lengthy prison sentences in federal institutions.

On behalf of the LAPD, Chief of Police William Bratton awarded the task force the Police Meritorious Unit Citation.

X-BOX OCDETF

In 2004, two Chinese nationals, a male and a female, left their home in Los Angeles and were driving eastbound through Kansas on Interstate 70. Their estimated speed when they attempted to make a left turn northbound on U.S. Route 281 was approximately 100 miles per hour. As a result, their black 4-door Lexus went airborne around 500 feet and flipped several times, landing upside down in a grassy field. The trunk opened and spilled 16 kilograms of cocaine and a bag containing over 68,000 ecstasy pills. The male driver had a fractured shoulder. The female was shaken but unhurt. The Kansas Highway Patrol turned the case over to the DEA Wichita Office, which reached out to me, and we formed the X-BOX OCDETF.

The pair driving illicit drugs from Los Angeles to the east coast was not unusual. To pay back their illegal immigration from the People's Republic of China to the U.S., they smuggled illicit drugs called "Riding the Snake."

The investigation into finding the source of the cocaine and ecstasy in Los Angeles led to a downtown business wherein liter-sized plastic containers of liquid P2P were boxed and labeled soy sauce and shipped from Shanghai to Los Angeles, Vancouver, Canada, and the Netherlands. P2P is used to manufacture methamphetamine and amphetamine. The Royal Canadian Mounted Police in Vancouver arrested four Chinese nationals and seized 2,000 liters of P2P, 80 pounds of ecstasy powder, a pill stamping machine, marijuana, cocaine, and $1 million in cash. Police in Holland seized 3,500 liters of P2P. In addition, the DEA encountered a Chinese national aboard a westbound Amtrak train from Chicago at Albuquerque, New Mexico, smuggling $750,000 in cash from the sale of P2P. The Chinese nationals were convicted and sentenced to lengthy prison terms in the U.S. and Canada.

Up in Smoke OCDETF

In 1996, California voters approved Proposition 215, "The Compassionate Use Act of 1996. The law permitted the use of medical cannabis to ensure seriously ill Californians have the right to obtain and use marijuana for medical purposes. A physician who has determined that the person's health would benefit from marijuana." Unfortunately, the act did not address medical marijuana facilities or sources other than an individual or caregiver being allowed medical marijuana. The law encouraged state and local governments to implement a plan to provide for the safe and affordable distribution of marijuana. Federal law prohibits the possession of marijuana for any purpose, including medical purposes.

On January 1, 2004, California Senate Bill 420 became law. It allowed patients to possess no more than eight ounces of dried marijuana and cultivate no more than six mature or twelve immature plants for personal use. It also encouraged counties and cities to retain or enact medical marijuana guidelines. As a result, in 2007, 70 cities and six counties established moratoriums on the medical use of marijuana; 38 cities and five counties banned the use of medical marijuana; and 24 cities and seven counties had established ordinances. The law also stated, "No individual or group can cultivate or distribute marijuana for profit."

An enterprising individual in Oakland, CA, created a pot university offering introductory and specialized training in creating a medical marijuana dispensary and technical positions in the marijuana trade, such as a "Budtender" earning $50,000 per year and top managers earning $100,000 per year.

Because Los Angeles County and the city of Los Angeles had no policy regarding medical marijuana, as a result, in 2005, entrepreneurs and criminals established over 400 medical marijuana dispensaries (which grew to over 600 by 2008), selling pounds of marijuana unabated. Additionally, hundreds of indoor and outdoor marijuana cultivation sites popped up. So naturally, everyone jumped into this new bonanza.

Medical practitioners also cashed in on the bonanza. The law stated no physician could be punished or denied any right or privilege for having recommended marijuana to a patient for medical purposes. Medical marijuana was supposed to treat cancer, anorexia, AIDS, chronic pain, spasticity, glaucoma, arthritis, migraine, or illness for which marijuana provided relief. Patients could record anything from pain wearing high heels to anxiety from school to obtain medical marijuana. The law required a patient to visit a doctor and get a medical marijuana recommendation before purchasing marijuana at a dispensary. The proposal was a letter or card and cost between $125 to $250. Next, a patient had to find a doctor who would prescribe marijuana. Only a few doctors would prescribe marijuana. The

Medical Board in California successfully prosecuted a doctor in northern California for fraud because he had patients sit before a television and watch a videotaped interview of the doctor asking questions. An average doctor sees 10-15 patients per day. The doctor reported on October 11, 2004, visiting 49 patients and grossing $7,350. During seven days, he saw 293 patients and grossed $43,950. Each patient filed an application, listed their ailment, paid $150, and received the recommendation.

A majority of owners of dispensaries used their businesses as an illegal front (criminal profiteering) to get marijuana to market, make huge profits, and provide a source for persons to get high under the guise of helping sick people. Dispensaries used sympathetic wording in their business names like "compassionate," "holistic," "herbal care," "spiritual," "wellness," and "caregivers," when in fact, they were purely in the business to profit from the illegal sales of marijuana. A medical advocacy website pointed out sales of marijuana would reach over $13 billion during 2006, up from $1.6 billion in 2005. Yet, Senate Bill 420 states medical marijuana is not for profit.

So naturally, everyone jumped into this new bonanza as the owner of a medical marijuana dispensary or a grower of marijuana. Rolling Stone magazine dubbed the proliferation of indoor grows "The California Weed Rush."

May 6, 2005 was my first encounter with a medical marijuana dispensary. Hollywood Division FES Detective Arturo Koenig called me to assist them with a search warrant at Compassionate Caregivers in West Hollywood, CA. Since 2004, Wilshire, Northeast, and Hollywood Division FES detectives have arrested people who bought pounds of marijuana and marijuana plants illegally from the dispensary.

The dispensary was like a fortress. Surveillance cameras covered every possible angle outside the dispensary to look for police or troublemakers.

Known to their customers as the "Yellow House" because of the exterior color of the former residence, Compassionate Caregivers was one of seven dispensaries with locations throughout California with one owner. Customers lined up around the block to buy numerous varieties of marijuana, hashish, edible marijuana, marijuana plants, oils, and other marijuana products. According to the owner's extensive financial records, from January 30 through November 1, 2004, the Yellow House grossed $1,979,321. During just one day, 302 sales netted over $50,000. The Oakland dispensary claimed to have 800 patients and earned $2 million during the same period.

Price boards lined one wall showing the cost of marijuana-laced medicine in increments of a half gram, one gram, and 8th of an ounce of several marijuana strains, hashish, kief, and edibles. For example, one-half gram of Granddaddy 'Purp' for $75, one gram of Willy's Wonder for $235, and an 8th of an ounce of Train Wreck for $400. One gram of Humboldt Melt concentrated hash sold for $30 and one gram of Budda's Sister kief for $25. Soda was $15, Carrot Cake $28, and Chocolate Turtles $10.

Receipts for the purchase of marijuana from growers showed marijuana was sold more at the dispensary than it cost on the street. For example, pounds of purple Kush cost $6,400, Afghan Haze was $4,800, and Star was $3,700.

During the search, officers arrested 14 but not the owner. In addition, the officers recovered cash hidden in ammunition cans, paper bags, drawers, and a duffel bag found throughout the four-bedroom house totaling $242,882. Detectives also found daily notations of receiving $250,000 per day.

Detectives also seized edible marijuana consisting of candy and soda manufactured by individuals and covert companies. The marijuana-laced edible candy and soda that had the same color packaging and product color as legitimate candy included: "Reefer's" peanut butter cups resembling "Reese's" peanut butter cups; "Rasta Pieces" as "Reese's Pieces"; "Kief Kat" as "Kit Kat"; "3 Rastateers" as "3-Muskateers bar"; "Stoney Rancher" as "Jolly Rancher Lollipops"; "Buddafinger" as "Butterfinger" candy bar; "Loopy Loops" as "Fruit Loops" cereal; "Trippy" as "Skippy" peanut butter; "Pot Tarts" as "Pop-Tarts"; and "Oeo" as "Oreo" cookies. Many illicit manufacturers produced products under unsanitary conditions, with no expiration dates, list of ingredients, and no danger warnings on the packaging. There have been instances wherein children and adults ingested edible marijuana and became very ill. I brought these products to the attention of corporate candy product manufacturers, who later brought infringement lawsuits against the edible manufacturers. An illicit marijuana-laced candy manufacturer was prosecuted successfully for infringement violations.

The next day, I wrote a search warrant and seizure order for the dispensary's bank accounts in Los Angeles and Oakland. At the Los Angeles bank, the dispensary's owner withdrew over $500,000 in cash stored in a safe deposit box before I got there. When I served the warrant in Oakland, the owner had just placed the money in a safe deposit box. I seized a total of $1,214,129 from the bank accounts.

The successful investigation of Compassionate Caregivers led, in part, to the creation of an OCDETF with the DEA, IRS, and LAPD named "Up in Smoke," targeting illicit medical marijuana dispensaries throughout Los Angeles, Oakland, and San Diego and numerous indoor and outdoor marijuana cultivation sites.

The task force targeted 63 dispensaries. Many dispensaries installed one-way glass windows at the entrance to a dispensary, along with surveillance cameras. In addition, all had safes to hold cash, marijuana, and weapons.

The task force served a search warrant at one dispensary with a glass front. After securing the business, one of the agents posed as the manager. A grower arrived at the dispensary and told the manager he had several pounds of marijuana for $2,500 a pound for Orange Kush. The manager ordered several pounds. Agents then arrested the grower after he returned to his truck and started to unload the marijuana. Agents then seized the van. An hour later, another grower entered the dispensary and asked the manager if he needed any marijuana. Agents arrested two more growers in the same manner.

Task force officers encountered in several dispensaries a six-page document that detailed guidelines and procedures to prevent the seizure of marijuana, cash, and documentation by law enforcement during a "raid." First, the sign read, "Before the raid, make the raid less successful. Store cash and marijuana off-site as much as possible." Next, during the raid, the people inside should be passive but not cooperate in the furtherance of the police investigation. Lastly, promote civil disobedience and do everything possible to prevent the police from performing their job. Take photographs and videos of the faces of the police.

Narcotics detectives estimated that over 600 homes in the San Fernando Valley were indoor cultivation sites. Without the owner's permission, renters of homes removed the flooring in rooms so they could grow marijuana indoors. An area the size of an average 20-foot by 20-foot garage could produce $1 million worth of marijuana. Heating lights, carbon dioxide generators, air purification units, humidity systems, blowers, and power cords overloaded the electrical wiring of homes. The growers dumped chemicals for growing marijuana into the soil and yards of a home. The watering of plants caused mold to spread throughout the houses. Unsuspecting property owners were shocked when detectives told them their homes were no longer livable and contained hazardous waste.

During 2005-2008, working with narcotics detectives throughout Los Angeles County, two detectives stood out. Eric Pierce and Toby Darby were two of the most knowledgeable detectives about marijuana cultivation. Together with them and others, we encountered numerous indoor marijuana cultivation sites in homes. Many of them tapped electricity before the meter. For example, one six-bedroom residence in the Hollywood Hills tunneled under the street and tapped into a high-voltage box. Another multi-story home in Woodland Hills tapped electricity underground to power 17 air conditioning units on three outside decks to maintain a 72-degree temperature in the numerous cultivation rooms inside the house. The growers camouflaged the tubing and the wiring for the 17 air conditioners with artificial ivy to resemble grape vines.

Inspectors with the Department of Water and Power monitored electrical power consumption. When a residence appeared to have excessive or no power usage, the inspectors passed the information to the task force. After visually checking a home, agents obtained a search warrant for a FLIR (Forward Looking

Infrared Receiver). Agents used a FLIR on a helicopter to measure the thermal imaging of a house. For example, during a flight, the observer aboard the aircraft noted the house was boiling on the imaging. In addition, the observer saw several homes in and around the place also displaying hot imaging.

An example of an indoor grow site, citizens complained about a neighbor named David they thought was involved in the illicit drug trade. An investigation by the LAPD Pacific Division Field Enforcement Section detectives found the windows in the house were all covered, and the roof's electrical wiring indicated he was 'tapping' (stealing electricity) before the meter. Detectives then obtained a search warrant and learned David was cultivating and processing marijuana in his house. He used each room of the house and attic to grow marijuana. In addition, David possessed methamphetamine, had several weapons, and receipts showing he grossed over $325,000 from marijuana sales. David converted the cash to money orders, cashier's checks, and bank checks to purchase land in Pennsylvania. Finally, David signed a confession wherein he admitted to growing marijuana for the past two years and selling marijuana to medical marijuana dispensaries and had stolen electricity for one year.

I obtained a search warrant for David's house for financial documentation regarding his marijuana sales. I found pages from a note tablet with David's writings, including "Is it safe to deposit 1,500 to 2,000 every other day at the bank," and "How to get cash in the bank without a red flag." These statements and receipts found for deposits and the purchase of money orders demonstrated David's understanding of money laundering. Money laundering is engaging in financial transactions to conceal the identity, source, and destination of money from a criminal enterprise. Section 186.10 of the California Penal Code defines the crime of money laundering: any person who conducts or attempts to conduct a transaction or more than one transaction within seven days involving a monetary instrument or instruments of a total value exceeding $5,000 or a total value exceeding $25,000 in 30 days, through one or more financial institutions (1) with the specific intent to promote, manage, establish, carry on, or facilitate the promotion, management, establishment, or carrying on of any criminal activity, or (2) knowing the monetary instrument represents the proceeds of or is derived directly or indirectly from the proceeds of criminal activity. For example, from November 19-December 17, 2004, David committed the crime of money laundering by structuring $51,100 in cash at two bank branches and purchasing money orders at a drug store and two U.S. Post Offices. In addition to money laundering, charged with grand theft for stealing 291,504 kilowatts totaling $34,954.

In 2007, the California Fourth District Court of Appeals, in a unanimous decision, overturned the conviction of an individual for possessing marijuana for sale. The Court overturned the case because the arresting officer did not have training or knowledge of the laws about medical marijuana. After that, I developed a training course on medical marijuana and presented it to law enforcement agencies throughout California.

On August 17, 2007, a complaining party emailed a complaint to the Los Angeles Police Commission against me. He alleged that I "...was violating an LAPD policy by spending too much of his workday on DEA issues. Packer participated in raids and was wearing DEA raid gear." The complaining party believed I was a zealot and should only work on Los Angeles and California issues, not federal ones. He further stated, "As a citizen and medical marijuana patient, I am concerned about this." The investigation went no further.

The task force served search warrants simultaneously at ten different medical marijuana dispensaries in Hollywood. At the same time, the Los Angeles City Council heard complaints from medical marijuana activists and others. My commanding officer was attending the City Council meeting. He called me on his cell phone and had me listen to what was happening in the forum. I heard shouts calling for the firing of Detective Dennis Packer.

On June 6, 2008, Tom La Bonge, Councilman for the 4th District, introduced a resolution regarding my upcoming retirement to the Los Angeles City Council. The Council then adopted the measure, and the Mayor and City Council extended their sincere appreciation for my loyalty, diligence, and dedicated service to the city and the Los Angeles Police Department. Finally, they extended their best wishes for health and happiness in the years ahead. In addition, the resolution included praise for my work with the Up in Smoke task force.

On January 31, 2008, the U.S. Attorney's Office (USAO) announced the ex-owner of Compassionate Caregivers pleaded guilty to federal drug distribution and money laundering charges, admitting he was responsible for more than 15,000 pounds of marijuana. Additionally, the owner admitted to selling over $95 million in marijuana from 2002-2005 at the seven marijuana stores and laundered over $50 million in drug proceeds. In addition, the USAO prosecuted two conspirators for money laundering. All three are serving terms in federal prison.

On December 8, 2008, John P. Walters, Director of National Drug Control Policy from the Office of the President of the United

States, presented the Up in Smoke task force with the Director's Award for Distinguished Service. The task force was awarded the honor at the White House.

Chapter 14

The Raiders and the Chargers

Los Angeles Raiders

After the 1981 National Football League season, the Oakland Raiders moved to Los Angeles and the Los Angeles Memorial Coliseum. The first home game as the Los Angeles Raiders was against the San Diego Chargers on November 22, 1982, after a 57-day player strike. John Ramsey was the stadium announcer, and I was the press box announcer. My job was to announce statistics, injuries, and other announcements to the news media and coaches in the press box. During the first quarter of the first game, Raiders Owner Al Davis went into the stadium announcer's booth and asked John if he was announcing the Los Angeles Rams and the Raiders. John answered he was announcing both teams. Mr. Davis wanted only one designated announcer for Raiders games, so John had to pick one or the other. John chose the Rams, as he had been with them for years. Then, Mr. Davis asked John to leave. The next thing I knew, I was the stadium announcer. I was fortunate that I had worked with John's spotters at Rams and USC games and could work with them without any problems. I announced the Raiders over the next 15 seasons, which included two years back in Oakland.

Figure 38: My supervisor in announcing Raiders games
was Al Davis' Executive Assistant, Al LoCasale. Al was
short in stature but had the presence of a giant.

My supervisor in announcing Raiders games was Al Davis'
Executive Assistant, Al LoCasale, who sat in the booth next to my
booth in the press box. Al spent more than three decades as Al
Davis' confidant from 1969 until his retirement in 2003. He was 82
when he passed away. Al was short in stature but had the presence
of a giant. Al was an assistant at USC, coached at the University of
Pennsylvania, and spent time coaching football during his stint in
the Navy. Next to my booth was the Owners Booth, often occupied
by Al Davis and his wife, celebrities, former football greats, and
security personnel. The security personnel were Bob Clark and
Earl Paysinger, both LAPD officers like me, who kept me updated
on who was in attendance. During one game, I had to use the

restroom badly and raced to the toilet during a time out on the field. The bathroom was to the left of the owner's booth. As I came out of my booth, Al Davis simultaneously came out of his booth, and we collided. I knocked him down. Bob and Earl waved me on. Upon returning to my booth, I asked Bob and Earl if I should offer an apology. They said not to worry about it. Al thought a linebacker hit him.

In my announcer's booth sat a red telephone. The only people who called me were Al Davis or Al LoCasale. I dreaded a call. Usually, the calls centered around not announcing a particular score by other teams or a milestone by an opponent. One time, the fans in the Coliseum were doing the "Wave" by standing up and raising their arms. The WAVE flowed around the stadium. The Raiders quarterback requested that I announce to the crowd not to do the Wave when the Raiders were on offense. I thought about the ramifications and bad press I would get if I made such an announcement. I thought for a moment and then did the only thing I could do, pray, and to my amazement, the crowd stopped doing the Wave.

To be a 'spot-on' and accurate announcer, you must know the game, the rules, the timing, and what is happening before you. Before games, I visited the official's locker room and discussed penalties with the officials and game operations. My favorite Referee was the late Mason L. "Red" Cashion and how he announced penalties with a Southern drawl. The fans, press, and officials demand accuracy in every announcement. In addition to the game, announcers have numerous commercials, which sometimes can be mind-boggling. In keeping track of everything football, I have told people, "An announcer is only as good as his spotters." My spotters consisted of three hand-picked people who know football per game. One spotter kept statistics, one kept track of the defense and tackles, and one monitored the offense and special teams, like return men, kickers, punters, long snappers, the backfield, and quarterbacks. Many of my spotters have been with me for decades. My regular spotters included Bob Richert, George L. Throop III, George Taylorson, and Brent Ferguson. My other spotters included Nick Rose, Joe De Ladurantey, Tom O'Brien, Steve Gillespie, Steve Quatro, Robin Mahkorn, Mike Chamberlain, Ken Johns, and Jim Ditmore. During one game, one of my spotters told me the ball was on the 52-yard line. Since the field only has a 50-yard line, I teased the spotter by asking, "Are you sure it's not on the 51-year line?" He then realized his mistake, and we got a big laugh out of it.

Figure 39: Announcing the Los Angeles Raiders with Spotters George L. Throop III, Joe DeLadurantey, and Bob Richert at the Los Angeles Memorial Coliseum.

On occasion, I got press credentials for special guests. However, some of those individuals almost got me fired for their actions. One person was Pastor James "Jay" Ahlemann. Pastor Jay was known for his ability to lead churches in dynamic growth in Tennessee, Arkansas, and Missouri. He had also been the chaplain for the then Washington Redskins and knew many players and coaches and the coach of the Raiders, Art Shell. Before games, my spotters would verify players and other information on the playing field or locker rooms. Pastor Jay accompanied my spotters and was expressly told by me not to go near the player's bench and certain areas of the field. During the first quarter, one of my spotters told me Pastor Jay was talking to Coach Shell at midfield. I grimaced as Al LoCasale walked toward him and then confronted Pastor Jay, and a conversation ensued. When Jay returned to my booth, I asked him what had happened with Al LoCasale. Pastor Jay said he was very friendly and asked who permitted me to be on the field. Jay said, "Dennis Packer did." I felt my career with the Raiders slipping before my very eyes. However, nothing further was said about it.

One person who was a significant influence on me during Raiders games was Lou McClary. Lou was the National Football League Security Representative and monitored each home game. On occasion, Lou would give me pointers on my announcing style, for which I was very grateful.

In the press box, I met and talked with other famous play-by-play broadcasters, including Dick Enberg, Merlin Olsen, Dan Fouts, Al Michaels, John Madden, Tom Kelly, Lee "Hacksaw" Hamilton, Hank Bauer, and the Pittsburgh Steelers' memorable commentator Myron Cope. Raiders' broadcaster Bill King was fun to know. He wore track shorts and sandals while announcing games at the Los Angeles Coliseum. Howard Cosell once said I was John Ramsey's illegitimate son.

Here's a riddle. I announced two football games in their entirety on the same day. One game started at noon and the other at 2:00 pm. How did I do it? On Sunday, January 18, 1991, I announced the Japan Bowl at noon. The game ended at 3:25 pm. After a 10-minute cab ride to the Yokohama heliport, Los Angeles Raider Coach Dan Connors and I helicoptered for 40 minutes across Tokyo to Narita International Airport. Japan Airlines then arranged for us to go through Immigration swiftly and to our flight to Los Angeles International Airport. After crossing the International Dateline, the flight landed on Sunday at 10:00 am. At 11:10 am, I arrived at the Los Angeles Memorial Coliseum to announce the Raider's playoff game against the Cincinnati Bengals at 2:00 pm. Thanks to my spotters, who kept me awake to announce the game. Later, Al Davis looked at me sternly and asked, "What if you had missed your flight?"

Oakland Raiders

In 1994, after 13 seasons at the Coliseum, the Raiders moved back to Oakland. I offered to continue to announce their games if they flew me up to Oakland. Al LoCasale appreciated the offer but declined, saying they would bring back their past announcer.

On September 17, 1995, the Oakland Raiders' first pre-season game was to take place versus the Kansas City Chiefs at the Oakland Alameda County Coliseum. Early that morning, I got a frantic call from Al LoCasale asking if I could announce the game.

Figure 40: Announcing the Oakland Raiders with Spotter George L.
Throop III at Oakland Alameda County Coliseum.

I was painting cabinets and relished the chance. He told me to report to the West Imperial Terminal at Los Angeles International Airport to fly with the team to Oakland. It turned out I got to sit on the plane next to Wide Receiver and now Hall of Famer Tim Brown.

Figure 41: Check out Tim Brown's eyes after a catch in this photo
shot by Jayne Kamin Oncea.

When we got to Oakland, I went up to the press box to check out
my booth from where I would announce the game. I looked down
at the field and saw the groundskeepers had painted the lines of
the football field in the wrong place and going in the wrong
direction. Because the Oakland Athletics baseball team was still
playing their games, the end zones were at home plate and center
field. The announcer's booth was in the same place as the baseball
stadium announcer, making it nearly impossible to see where the

football was during the game. And because they brought me up to Oakland alone, I had no spotters. I am thankful to this day for broadcaster Joel Myers, a former public address announcer, who, during his radio broadcast, knew my dilemma and let me know where the officials spotted the ball during each play. I followed his radio broadcast on every play and breathed a sigh of relief. After that, I was able to bring spotters with me. In subsequent flights in 1995, I had no problem recruiting spotters because we flew from Los Angeles to Oakland on Southwest Airlines with "Football's Fabulous Females," the Raiderettes, and bussed with them to the stadium. George L. Throop III and Bob Richert flew up with me, and my brother-in-law, Daniel Bosshart, who lived in Oakland, joined us. At the end of the 1996 season, I left the Raiders because of scheduling conflicts with my day job.

San Diego Chargers

In 1999, after announcing 22 seasons of San Diego Chargers and 25 seasons of Padre games, Robert Bruce "Bink" Binkowski became the Associate Director and, later, Executive Director (now retired) of the Holiday Bowl. The sponsors of the bowls asked Bink not to announce the Padres or Chargers. When Bink retired from the Padres, they held public tryouts to find a new announcer. Over 1,500 people auditioned by reading a 15-second commercial to help the Padres pick an announcer. According to the Padre staff, it was a zoo, and they could not find a suitable replacement. Thinking of the crowds at the tryouts, the Chargers dreaded the same thing might happen with their tryouts and reached out to Bink to see if he had any recommendations. Bink suggested me to the Chargers. Sean O'Connor, in charge of game day operations, then called me for a tryout. After that, I became the interim announcer for the Chargers. On game day, I drove from home to

San Diego with my spotters for 16 seasons, including 32 pre-season games, 128 regular season games, and two championship games. My primary spotters for the Chargers were George L. Throop III, Bob Richert, Brent Ferguson, Joe DeLadurantey, and Bud Grover. Announcing Chargers' greats included LaDainian Tomlinson, Phillip Rivers, Antonio Gates, and Junior Seau.

Figure 42: Announcing the San Diego Chargers at Qualcomm Stadium with Spotters George L. Throop III, and Brent Ferguson.

Three of my favorite announcements involved running back LaDainian Tomlinson. First, he set a team record for total yards from scrimmage, breaking his record of 2,172 yards. His eighth catch of the day gave him 100 for the season, making him the only player in NFL history to rush for 1,000 yards and catch 100 passes in the same season.

Figure 43: Chargers Spotters Joe De Ladurantey, me, and Bob Richert.

In 2017, the Chargers moved to Los Angeles, and I thought my drive would be shorter. Instead, the new game day operations director chose Eric Smith, with whom he had worked before, to be the stadium announcer. At one time, Eric, a local high school teacher, was my backup announcer for the Los Angeles Clippers. Eric is also the announcer for the USC Trojans.

NFLPA Collegiate Bowl

Since January 19, 2013, I have been the stadium announcer for the annual National Football League Players Association Collegiate Bowl. Members of the NFLPA select over 100 top NFL prospects from around the U.S. First, the players spend a week learning what it takes to be a professional NFL player, life skills, and financial preparedness. Next, they go through intense job interviews and resources the Player's Union offers. Then the players are divided into the National and American teams, coached by tenured NFL coaches, and played as an NFL game with NFL officials. My spotters are Bob Richert, Joe Figueroa, Jonathan Horowitz, John Jacobson, and George L. Throop III.

Chapter 15

Organized Crime and Vice Division

During my LAPD career, I never had the opportunity to work in a Vice Unit. However, I heard some interesting stories from one of my partners at North Hollywood Division, Mel Sandvig, who served tours in Vice, and after his LAPD career, became a lawyer and a Superior Court Judge. So, from March 2000, I worked alongside Organized Crime and Vice Division detectives and learned about vice laws and how they worked cases. In addition, I showed them how the financial investigation could enhance their chances of adding additional charges and confiscating their assets.

The laws targeting prostitution include Section 186.3(c) of the California Penal Code - All proceeds (assets) of a pattern of criminal profiteering activity, which property shall consist of all things of value that may have been received in exchange for the proceeds immediately derived from the design of illegal profiteering activity; 186.2 (a) PC Criminal profiteering activity wherein any act committed or attempted or any threat made for financial gain or advantage, which act or threat may be charged as a crime under the following: Section 186.2 (a) Criminal profiteering activity (12) from Pimping and Pandering; 186.10 (a) PC - Money Laundering; 14166 (c) PC – Structuring; and 19706 Revenue &Taxation Code - Tax Evasion.

Escort Services are business organizations that provide dates for paying clients but are often a legal front for sex work in locales where prostitution is illegal. Currently, Nevada is the only U.S. state to allow legal prostitution – in the form of regulated brothels. Police departments investigate prostitution using vice detectives.

A+ Escorts

In March 2000, "A+ Escorts," an out-call prostitution enterprise posing as a children's entertainment and party service, was formed by a convicted felon, his wife, and an 11-year veteran LAPD training officer. The trio pimped over 30 adult males and female prostitutes, who plied their illegal activity at various hotels throughout Los Angeles over the next 18 months. The criminal profiteering enterprise netted the trio over $324,500 until their arrests in August 2001. In addition, for financial gain, the trio allegedly utilized financial institutions to launder their illegal income through structured cash transactions to avoid detection.

In June 2001, vice detectives from the LAPD, Organized Crime and Vice Division focused their investigation on "A+ Escorts." The business also used the titles "A Plus Escort Service," "A Plus Male and Female Escort Service," "A Plus Group," and "A Plus Quality & Female Entertainers," which all were found under the heading "Escort Services" in the yellow pages of telephone books. Unbeknownst to a potential customer, the telephone number for one of the titles used the prefix '888' and a telephone number that automatically took the caller through a series of ring tones leading to the escort service. The purpose of the trunk lines and ring tones was to enable the caller to know if the caller was a private or business call. It also allows persons engaged in criminal activity, such as prostitution, to mask their illegal activity from detection by law enforcement.

On June 8, 2001, at approximately 8:00 pm, an OCVD male plainclothes detective, posing as a prostitution customer, telephoned the "A Plus Male and Female Escort Service" using an 888 number and arranged to have a woman come to a room at a hotel near Los Angeles International Airport. A male adult answered the call and identified himself as "Jason," a fictitious name, later identified as an 11-year veteran LAPD officer. Jason stated the rate for the woman's services was $200 cash for a one-hour massage and "companionship," but he would have to call back so he could check the woman's availability to serve him. At 9:00 pm, Jason called the customer back and stated a girl named, "Kristine," would arrive at the room in approximately 20 minutes. First, 'fictitious names' were typically used by men and women in prostitution. After the female came to the location, an undercover detective would obtain a 647(b) Penal Code violation (prostitution). No arrest was made due to the ongoing investigation—a prostitution complaint was completed detailing the incident for future prosecution.

On June 20, 2001, detectives obtained a search warrant for the subscriber information for the telephone using the 888 number. Upon serving the warrant, detectives learned the subscribed telephone number was "A Plus Escorts" and to a convicted felon who resided at an address in Harbor City, California. In addition, two of the trunk numbers were subscribed to a female at an address in Pico Rivera, CA. The service was activated on June 15, 2001. Detectives later learned that during a 48-hour period, 361 telephone calls had been called forwarded to the business. The pattern of rings was consistent with a prostitution organization masking itself as an escort service and using call forwarding to avoid police detection. The felon had been arrested in July 1997 for 266(f) PC (Pimping) while running "A Plus Escort Service" out of his residence in Harbor City, CA. The felon was also wanted on an outstanding warrant for selling a person for illicit purposes. Detectives also learned from the postal service the address in Pico Rivera was the primary residence of the female co-conspirator and the officer. The officer paid the home mortgage. Detectives also observed the officer at the place. Detectives learned A+ Escorts subscribed a telephone to the female co-conspirator. The telephone number had "Smart Ring Service," allowing the subscriber two rings, one type of ring for one number, and a different ring for another telephone number. The SRS enabled the subscriber to know if the caller was a private or business call. It also helped persons engaged in criminal activity, such as prostitution, to mask their illegal activity from detection by law enforcement. The officer and the co-conspirator received mail forwarded from their business address to their residence.

On June 26, 2001, at approximately 9:07 pm, an OCVD male detective in plainclothes, posing as a customer, telephoned the "A Plus Male and Female Escort Service." The detective arranged for a female to visit a hotel room near LAX. A female, identifying herself over the phone as "Katie," later identified as the female co-conspirator, answered the telephone call, and stated the charge would be $200 cash or $225 with a credit card. A couple of hours later, Katie arrived at the room. She asked the customer for his driver's license and imprinted his undercover credit card. The detective received a receipt written in the 'merchant blank' and asked the customer to fill out an information sheet. Katie then told her customer that she worked 'off-of tips' (additional money paid for sex) and performed full service, including oral copulation and sexual intercourse. Katie and her customer then discussed her and her company's sexual services. The detective obtained a 649(b) PC violation but did not arrest her due to the ongoing investigation. Katie then left the location.

In July 2001, detectives learned the officer was an 11-year veteran police officer assigned to Wilshire Division as their Training Coordinator on the day watch. Training coordinators maintain schedules of activities that affect officers in the Division, including monthly firearms qualification, training, and meetings involving officers and supervisory personnel. In addition, the officer purchased the house in Pico Rivera with his live-in girlfriend, who acted as a madame.

On five separate days from June through August 2001, detectives posed as customers of A+ Escorts and obtained violations of 647(b) PC. No arrest was made due to the ongoing investigation—a prostitution complaint was completed detailing each incident for future prosecution.

On August 22, 2001, one of the prostitutes made a tape-recorded telephone call to the owner and talked about performing intercourse and oral sex with the detective. The owner demonstrated his knowledge of prostitution activity. Detectives arrested the felon, madame, and officer for 266(h) PC (pimping). At the officer's residence, detectives served a search warrant and recovered several items, including the following:

- $7,000 in cash.

- An appointment book with the daily earnings of prostitutes from January through August 2001 and totals they earned each week, month, and year-to-date totals.

- A writing tablet containing customers' names, locations of hotels/motels, call-back telephone numbers, and the prostitutes dispatched to customers.

- File box containing 146 Bulls Eye credit card invoices with customer names, driver's licenses, and dates of birth. The customers were charged from $225 to $2,175 for sex with one or more prostitutes—the customers listed "entertainment" as the service performed.

In September 2001, LAPD Chief of Police Bernard Parks directed me to team with vice officers in conducting a financial review of A+ Escorts and the individuals involved. In the past, the proceeds (profiteering) of organized prostitution were not seized for asset forfeiture. In addition to nabbing their profits, detectives could use asset forfeiture to forfeit real property or other assets from pimps and panderers.

On September 12, 2001, I served the first of four financial search warrants, with the first at Wilshire Station. The other warrants were for the officer and Madame's Certified Public Accountant, the credit card company that processed charges for A+ Escorts, four financial institutions, and an escrow company.

The warrant served at Wilshire Station was for the officer's desk and his locker at Wilshire Station. On his desk was a large calendar with dollar figures of money deposited from prostitution. In addition, his locker identified a credit union where the officer banked.

The credit card company provided a two-page Merchant Application Agreement with the felon and his wife, dated March 1, 2000, listing the products/services sold by A Plus Escorts as "Children Entertainment" and "Party Services" at two different banks in Carson and Harbor City, CA. From May 2000 through July 2001 were 1,001 credit card purchases totaling $287,250. Additionally, the bank in Harbor City showed a total of $324,549 was processed from 1,001 credit card charges by prostitutes for "Entertainment Services" from April 7, 2000, through August 2001.

The officer's credit union account revealed he made 13 unusual cash deposits totaling $28,813 in nine days. Then on four days, he committed the felony crime of money laundering by depositing cash totaling $11,000 from April 30 through May 4, 2001. He deposited the money using Express Deposit Envelopes into an Automatic Teller Machine at Wilshire Station. Section 186.10 PC defines money laundering, a felony, as conducting one or more transactions exceeding $5,000 within seven days at a financial institution and knowing the cash represented proceeds from criminal activity. In addition, 14166(c) PC defines structuring as a felony, a person disguising a monetary instrument derived from illegal activity and conducting a series of transactions to avoid a Currency Transaction Report. The officer, madame, and felon were convicted and sentenced to prison. The officer also lost his LAPD job. Investigators suspected that as many as 28 escorts worked for the service.

Operation White Lace

On December 6, 2002, Los Angeles District Attorney Steve Cooley and LAPD Chief of Police William Bratton announced the arrests and indictments of five Russian immigrants following a 24-month investigation, dubbed "Operation White Lace," that uncovered one of the most prominent prostitution rings in Los Angeles history.

The investigation, which I was a member of, began in November 2000 by Los Angeles Police Department's Organized Crime and Vice Division after vice detectives located a two-page color advertisement for an escort service in the Pacific Bell Yellow Pages. Detectives knew from experience that these advertisements would cost escort services $10,000 or more per month, and even more. Russian Fortuna had advertisements in

Los Angeles, San Diego, San Jose, and San Francisco. They also publish advertisements in local newspapers such as the Beirut Times, Shalom L.A. newspaper, and the Los Angeles Russian Newspaper. Russian Fortuna advertisements directed clients to the website www.RussianFortuna.com Making Wildest Pleasures a Reality.

Later it was learned that Russian Fortuna was also known as "Russian Fortuna Tours," "Exclusive Girls Escort," "European Blondes," and "European Delight Escorts." The name, Russian Fortuna, was allegedly a travel agency in Russia run by the KGB. The opening website listed four headings with pictures depicting each service. The headings were "Limo Services, Hotel Reservation, Travel Tours, and Escort Services." Clicking a computer mouse on headings directed clients to Escort Services in every case. Escort Services prompted the client to choose either a blonde, a brunette, or a redhead. On the left side, the picture for one of these hair types brought up headshots (photos) of women. Clicking on one of the photos brought up a larger portrait or seductive photo of the prostitute, her first name, age, city where she resided in Southern California, and a telephone number.

Unbeknownst to a potential customer, calling the telephone number was a trunk line, which automatically took the caller through a series of ring tones leading to a woman who would answer the call as if she was the woman pictured on the website. She would then find pertinent information on the caller and direct them to a location near where the customer resided. Many of the telephone lines eventually connected to the dispatcher. The trunk lines and ring tones let madams know if the caller was a business call. It also enabled persons engaged in criminal activity to mask their illegal activity from detection by law enforcement. When the caller arrived at a woman's residence, they were confused because the woman answering the door was not the person pictured on the website. As we learned later, the web designer who created the website received numerous Russian fashion and pornographic magazines from the Madam of the organization. She would have the web manager cut out attractive women's photos and then scan or post them on the website as actual representations of the Russian Fortuna prostitutes.

Upon arriving at a prostitute's location, usually an apartment, they were met by a woman not pictured on the website. She would tell the customer she dyed her hair or explain why she looked different. The customer usually did not complain, especially after seeing such a beautiful woman. The Russian Mafia recruited women from one of the 14 former Soviet bloc nations. One prostitute came from as far away as Siberia. The women were exquisite, spoke good English, and were physically fit, refined, and well-educated. Upon being selected, they were flown to Los Angeles or illegally crossed the border into California from Mexico via persons working with the Madam. Many women, including the Madam, entered the U.S. as travelers from Moscow, Russia. They applied for a U.S. Government Form I-94 to study the English language at an English language center on Wilshire Boulevard in Los Angeles. The center's Executive Director allegedly accepted bribes from several individuals, including the Madam, who paid nearly $6,000 for a 12-month stay. Beverly Hills Police Department vice officers arrested three Russian women on separate days in 2001 for 647(b) PC – Prostitution. Each woman told officers they were Russian nationals and studying English. Detectives would later encounter the same women in the White Lace investigation. Many women posed as English language students and received an I-94 card to remain in the U.S. for up to one year. Some women married U.S. citizens, stayed indefinitely, or returned to their home countries.

To give legitimacy to Russian Fortuna Tours, Inc., the Madam registered the business with the California Secretary of State, listing her as the Chief Executive Officer, Chief Financial Officer, and Director. The Madam's daughter was the Secretary and Registered Agent of the business. The Madam had links to other Russians in Los Angeles who were experts at creating false identities, driver's licenses, and passports. Upon arrival, the Madam would distribute several pieces of fictitious identification to the women. These items included passports, UN driver's licenses, California Driver's Licenses, a fictitious Social Security Number, and credit cards in their new name. Each woman would use up as much credit as allowed on these cards and then trash them. Prostitutes, using fictitious names, were also signed up for California State Welfare as new immigrants and received as much as $452 monthly and food stamps until the balance paid out reached just under $49,000. This dollar figure arrived at because if the prostitute received more than $49,000 in benefits, they would be subject to a fraud investigation.

Then each prostitute was given an apartment to live and work in and had to report to one of five sub-madams. The Madam also provided prostitutes with health insurance and cosmetic surgery. Each sub-madam had a minimum of five prostitutes or more and kept track of the women's customers using computer-networked spreadsheets. At the end of the investigation, detectives seized the computer files containing 124 pages of spreadsheets containing 4,455 customers. Each customer on the spreadsheet contained their name, home or business address, telephone, Driver's License, credit card and number, the prostitute(s) they used, the sexual activities the customer chose, and how much they paid each time. Clients included doctors, lawyers, students, professional athletes, computer executives, judges, police officers, teachers, average persons, and students. One physician spent $30,000 for one night with nine women. Credit card receipts were intentionally mislabeled as driveway repairs or conference supplies to hide the charge. Aside from the spreadsheets were tally sheets and other documents written in Russian, which required translation. Detectives sought a translator from the FBI. The computer network enabled the Madam to keep track of each prostitute. One of the sub-madams was the daughter of the Madam, who resided at an apartment in North Hollywood. She had four different aliases and fictitious identification for each alias. The prostitutes learned that half of their wages would go to them, 50% to their respective sub-madam, and they had to eventually pay $10,000 back for their transportation to the U.S. For example, according to her records translated from Russian to English, a 31-year-old Russian national was sent to an apartment in Van Nuys, CA, and earned $26,870 from October 3-25, 2001. An alleged member of the Russian Mafia rented the apartment. A photo from the apartment showed her with one of the women arrested by the Beverly Hills Police Department. Because the money earned was tax-free, many women returned it to their extended families in Russia or the former bloc nations. The basic charge for 45 minutes of sex was $350 plus a tip of $100 or more. Customers could pay in cash or use a credit card(s). Additional charges were added from customers for extended periods and other sexual experiences. A male Russian national drove prostitutes to locations at hotels. This national married the Madam in a civil ceremony in Van Nuys in 1999.

On November 17, 2000, in an undercover operation, a police officer posing as a customer searched the Russian Fortuna website and saw a photograph of a woman named "Julia." The officer telephoned Julia's number on the website and asked for Julia. The dispatcher answered the telephone and said she was Julia. The customer then asked Julia to visit a hotel near Los Angeles International Airport. The prostitute was delivered to the hotel by a male Russian, who drove a car registered to his father, an alleged member of the Russian Mafia. The customer paid $300 using an undercover credit card swiped by the prostitute. She then gave the customer a credit card receipt, and the officer got a vice violation. She was not arrested because of the ongoing investigation. The same day, an undercover officer dialed the "Exclusive Girls Escort 24 Hours 365 Days" telephone number, which was forwarded to another telephone number. The dispatcher answered the third number. A search warrant revealed the number was at an apartment on North Doheny Drive in West Hollywood. The Madam and her daughter rented the apartment, and the utilities were under the name of a sub-madam.

On March 8, 2001, an undercover officer called a "European Delight Escorts 24 Hour 7 Day Service" telephone number. A search warrant revealed the address for the telephone number of an apartment on N. Oakhurst in Beverly Hills. The sub-madam from the apartment on North Doheny leased the Oakhurst apartment. The apartment manager identified a photo of the sub-madam with a different name. Long Beach Police Department vice officers arrested the sub-madam for 647(b) PC prostitution, wherein she used another name. A call to Lana at "European Delight Escorts 24 Hour 7 Day Service" was found to be an apartment on South Hauser Bl, Los Angeles. The Madam leased the apartment, and the sub-madam from Oakhurst paid the utilities.

Fifteen more undercover calls identified four flats in San Francisco, 42 apartments in Southern California, members of the Russian Mafia, and other persons involved in the conspiracy.

In late August and early September 2001, a rival prostitution organization committed a series of crimes to take control of Russian Fortuna Tours, including a home invasion robbery and a kidnapping for ransom. All of the suspects were arrested, convicted, and sentenced to prison. The husband of the daughter of the Madam reported the kidnapping. The daughter was also found to be a sub-madam and arrested for 266(h) PC Pimping-for handling six prostitutes.

On October 21, 2001, the task force searched 18 apartments rented or leased by Madam. One of the apartments in Hollywood was a prostitute who earned $153,093 over ten months. In another apartment, detectives found 84 credit card receipts. One customer was charged $17,407 for three days of prostitution services. Several thousand dollars in cash and 832 documents provided evidence that was the basis for additional search warrants for 41 businesses, 48 bank accounts, and ten residences in Los Angeles and San Francisco.

By triangulating cell telephone records, detectives could locate three parking structures in San Francisco to find the Madam's automobile. Detectives found the car, and the alarm was activated. The parking attendant notified her to turn off the alarm. When she arrived, detectives took her into custody. The Madam's roommate saw the arrest from an upper apartment window and tried to drop a Christmas tree out the window on the detectives as they entered the apartment building. She was arrested. A search of the apartment revealed that the Madam was going to move her business to San Francisco and change the name from Russian Fortuna to "Fine Antiques Inc."

Grand Jury indictments, returned October 24, 2001, were made public when five of the six defendants were arraigned and pleaded not guilty to conspiracy, pimping, pandering, and money laundering. The ringleaders allegedly employed 28 female Russian nationals and earned an estimated $5 million to $8 million during 22 months of illegal activities in Los Angeles and Beverly Hills. The six task force members and I received LAPD's Police Meritorious Unit Citation.

Chapter 16

Other Opportunities

After becoming John Ramsey's backup voice, all kinds of announcing opportunities opened up for me. Here are some of the other opportunities that came my way.

Los Angeles Skyhawks

In 1978, Joe Buttitta, the radio play-by-play voice of the Los Angeles Skyhawks of the American Soccer League gave my name to John Hubbard, Operations Manager for the Skyhawks. That recommendation resulted in announcing their games at Pierce College Stadium in Woodland Hills. I announced the Skyhawks for two seasons.

LAPD Centurions Football

From 1979 through 2021, I was the game announcer for the LAPD Centurions football team who played in the National Public Safety Football League. The team consisted of police officers, some with prior football experience in college and the pros, and amateur players. The games benefited the Blind Children's Center of Los Angeles. In Super Police Bowl I, the Metro-Miami Magnum Force defeated the Centurions 24-21 at the Los Angeles Memorial Coliseum. Each season, games were played at various college and high school stadiums. The biannual Centurions versus the Los Angeles City Fire Department was always an exciting game. Teams from the NYPD (New York Police Department) and NYFD (New

York Fire Department) were also spirited games. My spotters were Bob Richert, Joe Figueroa, and Bud Grover. I also groomed new game announcers during these games, such as former Los Angeles Raiders defensive back Ronald Calvin Foster who now announces the Centurions and St. John Bosco high school football.

Black Tie Security

Lou McClary provided security for the Friars Club Celebrity Roasts and awards banquets at hotels in Beverly Hills. Lou formed a cadre of off-duty LAPD officers, of which I was fortunate to be a member, wearing a black tie (tuxedo). Our presence at events reassured patrons of their safety and kept the paparazzi nearby. On one occasion, I escorted actress Elizabeth Taylor. On another, I guarded Austrian Holocaust Survivor, Nazi hunter, and author Simon Wiesenthal.

Jay Johnstone

In 1982, during a pregame at Dodgers Stadium, major league baseball outfielder Jay Johnstone pulled one of his infamous pranks on me. A ballplayer's name on the starting lineups for the visiting team was hard to pronounce. I made the mistake of walking over to the visitor's dugout and asking a coach how to pronounce a name. The coach directed me to a person on the bench. I asked that person how to pronounce a player's name. He told me the pronunciation. I then went back behind home plate and announced the starting lineups for the visitors. After announcing the player's name, I got hit in the butt by a baseball. It stung. Then, the player approached me and demanded to know who told me to pronounce his name that way. I pointed to the coach on the bench. The player said, "He's not a coach. That's Jay Johnstone."

Stu Nahan and Jim Hill

August 7, 1984, as a favor for USC Baseball Coach Rod Dedeaux, I announced the Japanese All-Stars versus the U.S. Collegiate All-Star players' championship baseball game at Dodger Stadium. Part of my announcing chores was introducing the coaches and players from both teams. After completing the introduction of both teams, including their names, position, and city or town from where they were from, I breathed a sigh of relief. Sportscasters Stu Nahan and Jim Hill approached me while shaking their heads negatively. I asked what was wrong. Stu then told me that I had mispronounced one of the Japanese player's name's and said an expletive instead and how embarrassing it was to Japan and the U.S. The player's last name was "Fukumama." I was crestfallen but felt I did not say what Stu said, but Jim followed him. After the game ended, I rushed down to the videographer's room and had him playback the introduction of the starting lineups. I listened closely, and I did not say what Stu had said. I said the name correctly. A few days later, Stu drove past the Police Academy behind Dodger Stadium. I knew two motorcycle officers who stopped Stu and made him think he was going to jail. As Stu begged forgiveness, a black and white police car drove up to take him to jail. I got out of the vehicle and approached Stu. He then realized the joke was on him and breathed a huge sigh of relief.

UCI Bren Center

January 8, 1987, was the opening night of the University of California Irvine Donald Bren Events Center. I announced the first Anteaters basketball game against the Aggies of Utah State. On January 29, I was also the announcer for the Anteaters game versus the University of Nevada Las Vegas Rebels.

Coaching Soccer

In 1989, I coached the AYSO Region 2 Boys, Age 6, Grasshoppers. The team of twelve boys had eight wins, three losses, and one tie, scoring 45 goals and only giving up 19 goals. My son Brett played forward, midfielder, and sweep. When the team played indoor soccer, they won two games and lost one.

Voiceovers

In 1989, I performed a voiceover for a commercial promoting Cache, a Latin Club and restaurant in Los Angeles.

In 2005, one of the producers of Sony Computer Entertainment America Inc., heard me announcing the Chargers and asked me to perform as the game announcer for their video game, "Road to Sunday." My voiceover would be heard if the gamer wanted ambient sounds of the game. My script for the recordings had over 3,500 lines, many of which were recorded in several different ways. Recording sessions were a total of four hours per day with breaks and lunch. All readings were recorded in a sound stage and had to be at the same modulation (sound level). A sound engineer stood by to monitor the recordings and direct announcements. For example, one set of announcements was, "A gain of one yard." "A gain of two yards." "A gain of three yards" and so on up to 110 yards. Then, I had to do another set of announcements about the loss of yardage. "A loss of one yard." "A loss of two yards." And so forth, up to 110 yards. Next was scoring announcements. "Los Angeles 2, Los Angeles nothing." "Los Angeles 3, Los Angeles 4." "Los Angeles 5, Los Angeles 6." The score went up to 90 points and included all NFL teams read first by the city and then by their name. "Rams 2, Rams nothing," and so forth. Then scoring was announced with the city and name, i.e., "Los Angeles Rams 2, Los

Angeles Rams nothing." Player announcements had at least 14 reads, i.e., "John Smith with the catch," "Pass intended for John Smith," "John Smith with the interception," "John Smith with the fumble," "John Smith receives the kickoff," "John Smith returns the punt," and so forth. I was also called back in the following years to update players and teams.

Los Angeles Clippers Basketball

From 1990-2002, I was the game announcer for the Los Angeles Clippers. The Clippers played games at the Los Angeles Sports Arena, Honda Center in Anaheim (1994-1999), and Staples Center (Crypto.Com) in Los Angeles. The 1991-1992 season saw the team go to the first round of the playoffs for the first time in 16 years, but they lost against the Utah Jazz. The Clippers made the playoffs the following year but lost to the Houston Rockets in the first round. As everyone knows, professional basketball is exciting to watch as a lot is happening every second, and you must keep your eye on the ball. For example, if a player commits a foul, the game announcer must know the rules and signals of the officials on the court. The announcer must quickly announce who fouled, how many fouls that player has, the number of team fouls, and how many shots a player can take. If there are substitutions, the announcer must give the names of who is coming and going out. All these actions can co-occur. At halftime, the game announcer must provide the scoring by players on both teams immediately.

In his "Notes on a Scorecard," Sportswriter Allan Malamud wrote about Dominique Wilkins' debut as a Clipper. 'NIQUE' bellowed Dennis Packer after Dominique scored a basket (Dominique preferred NIQUE). Malamud further wrote, "Dominque is such a great name. There is no need to shorten it. I don't care what his nickname is, "DOMINQUE" would be beautiful music to my ears."

I sat at center court with Clippers Game Operations Directors Lou Rosenberg, Leslie Murrota, and Erin Wolfe-Beyer, on my right, who provided commercial announcements to make throughout the game. On my left was Kent McLaren, the Official Scorer. Next to him were the Timer and Scoreboard Operator Kyle Lucas and 24-Second Clock Operator Tony Monton. Kent said, "To be a successful announcer you have to have a 'real feel' for the game, great timing, and work hand-in-hand with the Official Scorer,

Figure 44: Announcing the Los Angeles Clippers with Official Scorer Kent McLaren and Statisticians Kevin Hill, Genene Levy Turndorf, and Dave Davis.

Timer, and 24-second clock Operator while following the action on the court."

Most of the National Basketball Association officials were very professional and friendly, but Dick Bavetta and Joey Crawford were authentic favorites of mine. They made it a point to converse about the game with the official scorer and me throughout the games. Both men made you feel like you were a critical part of the game. I remember Joey Crawford maintaining eye contact with me whenever he blew his whistle or signaled a foul or basket. I loved how Joey would get on his tiptoes running near the baskets. Dick's signals were clear and deliberate. Sometimes, he would come to the table and explain a call. Joey officiated over 2,500 games in his career. Dick holds the record for most officiated games with 2,635 and retired in 2014.

Donald Sterling, then, the owner of the Clippers, sat directly across the court from me. The Raiders owner, Al Davis, would sit with Mr. Sterling when the Raiders were in town. In one Clipper game, Al sat by himself. During the play, Al got up from his chair, walked directly across the court, greeted me, and shook my hand. He told me he missed me up in Oakland. He then turned and returned to his seat. The officials stopped the play, approached me, and asked what Al was doing. I told them he did not like the way the game was going. The officials then went over to Al and consoled him. After that, the game went on without further ado.

My favorite Clippers players were from the 1997 team of Charles Outlaw, Brent Barry, Rodney Rogers, Loy Vaught, and Malik Sealy.

After ten seasons, April 12, 2002, was my last night announcing the Clippers. It was the ninth sellout of the season with a crowd of 18,964, which tied a franchise record versus the San Antonio Spurs.

Master of Ceremony

From 1991 through 2006, I was the Master of Ceremonies for the Los Angeles Police Revolver and Athletic Club Sports Awards Banquets at the Los Angeles Police Academy.

Figure 45: Master of Ceremony with LAPD
Chief of Police Daryl F. Gates.

Starting in 1985, LAPD officers who were near retirement asked me to be the Master of Ceremonies for their retirement luncheons or evening get-togethers. In preparation for these events, I had fun researching their backgrounds from birth through their retirement. I then added humor and props. For example, at one retirement luncheon, I made a life-size outline of the honoree and added parts of his body wherein he was injured or impacted during his career. At another luncheon, the officer was in several traffic accidents during his career, and so I displayed a smashed police vehicle door. In addition, I wore a tuxedo shirt and jacket and black shorts for some luncheons. I was the MC for over 50 retirements.

In 1990, I performed the eulogy at John Ramsey's memorial service.

February 13, 2001, I was the MC for the Trojan Club of the San Fernando Valley and Ventura dinner honoring Dr. Arthur C. Bartner, Director of the USC Trojan Marching Band.

At the Cerritos Center for the Performing Arts, I was the background announcer for the "America the Beautiful" Concert performed by the Trojan Marching Band under the direction of Dr. Arthur C. Bartner.

From 2004 through 2007, I was the MC for the San Gabriel Valley Council of the Boy Scouts of America's annual Sports Breakfast. This fundraising activity provided camps for young boys and men. Honorees included Mike Schlappi, four-time Paralympic medal winner; Hall of Fame Jockey Chris McCarron; and former Dodger pitcher Jim Gott.

The Mighty Ducks

After a four-year absence from the National Hockey League, I became a Cast Member--public address announcer for a new team--The Mighty Ducks of Anaheim. I was given a Disney ID Name Tag with the Ducks logo and "DENNIS" printed on the tag. Opening night was Thursday, September 16, 1993, at the Ducks' home ice at the Arrowhead Pond of Anaheim.

The official opening night of season play was October 8, 1993, vs. the Detroit Red Wings. It was a significant production and one you will not forget. As the arena darkened before the game, I announced to the crowd while a video played on giant overhead scoreboards:

"There's fire in their eyes you'll see them.

Challenging the odds, they'll beat them.

Power mixed with pride unleash it.

Danger on the ice besiege it."

Then I proclaimed: The Mighty Ducks of Anaheim!

The crowd responded: Rock the Pond!

I again proclaimed: A surge of force that never dies.

The crowd responded: Rock the Pond!

Finally, I proclaimed: The Mighty Ducks of Anaheim!

The crowd responded: Rock the Pond!

A surge of force that never dies.

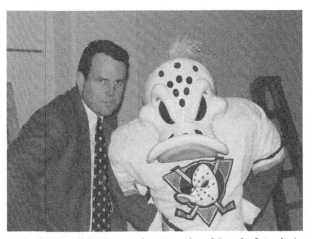

Figure 46: With Wild Wing at the Arrowhead Pond of Anaheim.

January 24, 1994, issue of The New Yorker reported each game at the pond was riveting as a "V" formation of flying ducks dive bomb a goalie, and then Wildwing (the Mighty Ducks mascot) dropped down from the ceiling on a cable to the ice during the playing of the haunting Latin cantata "Carmina Burana," thundering over the sound system. As Wildwing hits the ice, the announcer proclaims, "In a monster-truck voice intones, Ladies and gentlemen, your Mighty Ducks of Anaheim."

The article further described, "...your Decoys, as the Anaheim announcer calls them, in one of those deep, rumbling monster-truck-rally voices, as eight multiculturally appropriate young women, clad in tiny purple-jade-silver-and white uniforms, who perform Disney choreographed skating routines--whirling and leaping and waving hockey sticks--before every game and between periods after twin-Zambonis have speedily cleaned the ice."

September 21, 1993, Los Angeles Times Sports Reporter Allan Malamud, in his "Notes on a Scorecard," wrote, Pittsburgh Penguin defenseman Marty McSorley to former King public address announcer Dennis Packer during one of McSorley's visits to the penalty box Saturday night at Anaheim Arena, "It's been so long since I've seen you at a game. I just wanted to spend some time with you."

During the final games of the inaugural season, long-time Disney cast members visited my announcing booth to learn about how I conduct games.

At the end of the season, the Chairman of the Ducks, Michael Eisner, summoned me to his office with the President of the Ducks, Antonio Tavares. They presented me with a plaque with the inscription, "Presented to Dennis Packer for your hard work and dedication in building the MIGHTY DUCKS professional sports franchise in record time. You are recognized as a member of our inaugural team that has begun a tradition of success that will continue through the years." After receiving the plaque and a photograph of the staff, they let me go.

Miss Orange County Pageant

Figure 47: Master of
Ceremonies to crown
Miss Orange County 1994.

March 19, 1994 was "A Greek-Roman Evening" at Orange Coast College, where I was the master of ceremonies for the selecting Miss Orange County 1994. I borrowed a marching band's drum major costume, with leather sandals, skirt, breastplate, and helmet. Of course, I had to spray my white legs brown to look natural. My opening line was, "The Great Roman Empire of Orange County is blessed with such beautiful contestants. We will enjoy the festivities with all the gods on Mt. Olympus and wait to see which of our goddesses will be crowned."

XV FIFA World Cup

Figure 48: During the FIFA World Cup at the Rose Bowl in
1994, the voice of the USC Trojans Pete Arbogast and I
shared the announcing chores for many of the semifinal
matches.

From June 17 through July 17, 1994, USC football's voice, Pete
Arbogast and I shared announcing soccer matches for the XV FIFA
World Cup at the Rose Bowl. Pete and I shared the USA vs. Mexico
match. My preliminary games included Cameroon vs. Sweden,
Romania vs. Colombia, Romania vs. Argentina, and the final,
Brazil vs. Italy, won by Brazil 3-2 in a dramatic penalty kick
showdown.

The hardest part was learning the correct pronunciation of the
players' names. For example, 17 of the 22 players on the Brazil
team used multi-syllable first names like "Ro-NOL-do," "Bran-
co," and "HOR-HEE-YO."

Ice Dogs

I announced the inaugural season of the Los Angeles Ice Dogs in Los Angeles 1995-1996 at the Los Angeles Memorial Sports Arena. My daughter Natalie walked and babysat the English Bulldog mascot at home games. However, they moved due to poor attendance at the Long Beach Sports Arena.

NCAA Division I Men's Basketball Championship

I was the game announcer for the 1998 NCAA Division I Men's Basketball Championship West Regional at the Arrowhead Pond of Anaheim.

Tournament of Roses

December 31, 1999, I was the announcer for the Rose Bowl Game Kickoff Luncheon and Hall of Fame. I also announced the 2000 Tournament of Roses queen and court coronation.

U.S. Soccer Federation

January 16, 2000, I was the game announcer for the U.S. Soccer Federation "International Friendly" soccer game between the United States of America and the Islamic Republic of Iran at the Rose Bowl. The Iranian names were a real challenge.

Kart Racing

On weekends in 2001, at the request of Jayne Oncea, I announced Kart Racing at Irwindale Raceway. There were up to 11 races each day involving different age brackets from 5-21 years of age. Some races included Senior Can, Kid Karts, Shifters, Junior Super Box, and Super Port.

Battle of the Sexes Gender Bowl

On August 23, 2005, I announced the first-ever Gender Bowl exhibition football game at the Los Angeles Memorial Coliseum. The Orange County Breakers, a National Women's Football Association professional female football team, squared off against an all-male "Over 30" group "who never realized their dream of playing pro football."

Officiant

On March 15, 2020, Christian Global Outreach certified me as an Officiant to perform marriage ceremonies in California. On May 15, 2021, I was the Officiant for Trent and Kathleen Richert's wedding. I also researched and wrote their vows.

Chapter 17

Federal Service

I have always believed in the words attributed to Edmund Burke, 1729-1797, "The only thing necessary for the triumph of evil is for good men to do nothing." Hence, my 35+ years with the LAPD, nine years with the DEA, and four years as a government contractor.

Figure 49: Chief of Police William Bratton presented me with a certificate commemorating 35 years of service with the LAPD.

During the 19 years I worked at Narcotics Division, I thoroughly enjoyed working alongside special agents from the DEA, FBI, BATF, Internal Revenue Service, Immigration and Naturalization

Service, DSS, and Homeland Security. On June 30, 2008, I retired from the LAPD, but I still felt interested in drug enforcement work from a different perspective--intelligence. However, I was too old to be an agent, so a year before my LAPD retirement, I applied for an Intelligence Research Specialist (IRS) position with the DEA in Los Angeles. The mission of the DEA is to reduce the availability of illicit drugs in areas and communities in the U.S.

An IRS supports special agents and police officers with counter-drug investigations by analyzing information, identifying drug trafficking organizations, providing reports, and other visual and written media. IRS analysts also access numerous law enforcement, public, and privatized databases to research drug targets. Analysts also attend confidential source debriefings and write reports as needed.

DEA Intelligence Research Specialist

On October 31, 2007, the DEA tentatively selected me for the position of Intelligence Research Specialist, GS-0132-13, the highest step to begin working at the Los Angeles Field Division. Accordingly, on July 21, 2008, I reported for duty to the LAFD, Intelligence Group 3, at the Southern California Drug Task Force (SCDTF)/Los Angeles High-Intensity Drug Trafficking Area (HIDTA) in the Rampart Area of Los Angeles. Congress created HIDTAs in the Anti-Drug Abuse Act of 1988 to assist federal, state, local, and tribal law enforcement agencies throughout the U.S. with task forces to combat drug trafficking.

I was fortunate because I previously knew many agents, police officers, and civilian support staff during my years with the LAPD and serving on task forces. Now, I was on the other side of investigations in a position to use government databases I previously did not have access. The financial crimes network was one of the most critical databases. The data from the system enabled me to enhance money laundering and drug trafficking cases. I also had access to investigations throughout the world.

My first duty assignment was Intelligence Group 3 at the SCDTF. My mentors were Supervisory Intelligence Research Specialist (GS) Gerri Fowler and IRS analysts Elizabeth "Liz" Sotomayor and Eric Bernard. Gerri had many years with the DEA and had a friendly and straightforward leadership style. She was open to ideas, and her encouragement brought out the best in the Group. Liz held her own with agents and officers, and her organizational and research skills were second to none. With the number of task forces in the SCDTF/HIDTA, it was easy to get sidetracked. Liz demonstrated to me how to organize an investigation, how to file reports and documents, and the means to target drug traffickers. She was well-respected by agents and task force officers. Eric, now a supervisor of Intel Group 2, was the commiserate analyst. His experience with an intelligence agency in Langley, Virginia, and foreign assignments made him the go-to analyst for ideas on tackling an investigation. He reminded me of the adventurer Indiana Jones.

After five months of working on cases, IRS analyst Marilyn Escalante, from the Riverside District Office, and I shipped off to the Basic Intelligence Research course at the DEA's Quantico Training Academy. Class No. 62 course of instruction was from January 5 through April 10, 2009. The para-military intelligence training had us wearing green uniform shirts, khaki pants, and boots or tennis shoes. Nineteen analysts, consisting of 13 women and six men, started the course, and 18 graduated. Analysts came from DEA offices in Los Angeles, El Paso, Laredo, New York, Little

Rock, Washington, D.C., and the Caribbean. Roger Case, the analyst from Arkansas, had served in law enforcement and was TFO like me.

Classes were structured like college lecture courses, except the class had to stand at attention before class, greet the instructor and then stand at attention after classes had ended. In addition, each class had a Section Chief, a Unit Chief, a coordinator—we had two—and two experienced IRS analysts who served as class mentors and regularly met with students to monitor their progress. The Section Chief, Unit Chief, and coordinators handled discipline.

The DEA Academy and FBI Academy are located within the confines of the U.S. Marine Corps Quantico Military Base. The base has several active Marine Corps schools with active-fire training and movement of tanks and other military equipment. As a result, the DEA buildings shook from the repercussions of artillery and weapons firing. After the first two weeks of training, students were allowed to go to the military base commissary stores and restaurants, the FBI Academy, or go no more than a 25-mile radius off base to surrounding communities. The DEA provided vans to go to the base amenities, FBI Academy, Metro transportation facilities, or neighboring cities for shopping and sightseeing. Someone at the DEA Academy thought they saw me in a government van near Valley Forge, Pennsylvania, 250 miles from the Academy, which would have been a serious violation of the 25-mile radius rule.

One of the class coordinators thought he had me dead to rights. The pool of government vans all looked alike. Earlier that day, I signed out of a van and noted the odometer miles as I did every time, I used their vans. I then took five students to a Metro Stop

10 miles away. Upon my return at the end of a trip, I recorded the mileage when I returned the vehicle. Unfortunately, the coordinator should have checked the miles each way and the van I used, which cleared me of the accusation. In addition, there are cameras everywhere in the Academy classrooms, hallways, corridors, and offices to monitor staff and students 24 hours a day. A law instructor overheard the advisor's miscue. To rub it into the coordinator, the instructor walked by and said, "Thanks, Dennis, for the Valley Forge sweatshirt."

On March 25, 2009, our class had firearms training at the FBI Academy range. Although analysts do not carry or fire weapons in the line of duty, we received firearms safety and handling instructions if we came in contact with a firearm. Then we got the chance to fire on the range, semi-automatic pistols, AR-15 rifles, and a shotgun. Some of the students staggered backward after firing the shotguns. We also got to hold and fire a classic, a "Tommy Gun," a Thompson caliber .45 Sub-Machine Gun, the signature weapon of outlaws in the 1920s, and used by federal agents.

Before graduating, our class held a farewell dinner on the ground floor at the memorable Quantico USMC Museum. The museum is spectacular. In the middle of the ground floor was a conning tower from an aircraft carrier. Adjacent to our tables were actual scenes from battles with a tank and military vehicles from World War II and a Sikorsky helicopter from the Korean War. Jets and other aircraft were suspended from the ceiling.

On April 10, 2009, 17 classmates and I, as Class No. 62, graduated from the Academy at the DEA Headquarters auditorium. Acting Administrator Michele M. Leonhart administered the Oath of Office to us and presided over the ceremony.

Figure 50: On April 10, 2009, I graduated with DEA Intelligence Research Specialist Class No. 62. As part of the ceremony the Acting Administrator, Michelle M. Leonhart, presented each analyst with our government credentials.

Upon my return to Los Angeles, I continued to work with Intel Group 3 and was asked to conduct training. Wouldn't you know it, all agents and IRSs are required to attend the Instructor Development Course at the DEA Academy at Quantico. In early February 2010, I attended the training. When I arrived, it was bitterly cold, and the talk was about an impending snowstorm. On Friday morning, February 5, it began to snow. At noon, the Academy staff excused everyone who lived within a 50-mile radius of Quantico. The Academy staff did leave us a skeleton crew of commissary workers and a cook. However, for those of us from California, Texas, and homes outside the 50-mile radius, we had to hunker down until the storm passed. That night though, it snowed even harder. By Saturday afternoon, the snow was over 30 inches deep burying cars in the parking lots, and snow piled against doors made it almost impossible to go outside.

On Sunday, we rewired the antenna for a large television in one of the classrooms to enable us to watch the Super Bowl. The following week, the academy was closed. Food was scarce in the cafeteria, so we were careful to make the food last until the emergency was over. I tried to arrange a flight home, but the roads were impassable—instructors road snowmobiles to the campus. On February 9 & 10, while 46 inches more snow fell, we finished the course with only a handful of students. Weather services named the onslaught of snow "Snowmageddon." The roads and parking lots were piled high with snow from snowplows. On the 12th, the skies were finally clear, and I thankfully got the first flight out of Dulles Airport to fly home.

Two years later, I transferred to Intelligence Group 4 at the LAFD called "Collections," led by Supervisory Intelligence Research Specialist David A. Stinnett, who inspired analysts to conduct long-term research, write reports, and work on specialized projects. However, we did not support investigations.

One of my primary assignments was identifying and researching Consolidated Priority Organization Targets or drug kingpins, which comprise the leaders of the most prolific drug trafficking and money laundering organizations with the most significant impact on the U.S. illicit drug supply. There are CPOTs worldwide, of which roughly 40 affect the LAFD. I was shocked to find the parent of a kingpin lived right around the corner from my residence. I wondered if the kingpin ever visited his mother. The kingpins are mainly from Mexican, Central American, and Colombian cartels. My research included their backgrounds, extended family, locations, associations, and relationships with individuals in the U.S. To further my research, I traveled to Mexico City. At the American Embassy, I interviewed intelligence analysts from the Mexican federal police about the cartels and kingpins. These analysts had a different perspective on drug trafficking in Mexico.

DEA Supervisory Intelligence Research Specialist

On March 30, 2014, after receiving a Certificate of Appreciation from the Executive Office of the President of the U.S. and DEA Exceptional Performance Awards for intelligence work, I was promoted to a GS (Supervisory Intelligence Research Specialist) for Intelligence Group 3 at the SCDTF. I then switched to Intel Group 2 at Division. Intel Group 2 consisted of seven highly skilled IRS analysts, four serving the Los Angeles office and three at the Riverside District Office. The enforcement groups at both locations held these analysts in high esteem.

Newly appointed supervisors must attend the Supervisor Development Institute at the DEA Academy within the first year of being promoted. Accordingly, from May 27 through June 4, 2015, I attended Institute No. 87 at the DEA Academy. Thankfully, there was no snow.

One of my most dedicated analysts at the Los Angeles office, Duke, also serves in intelligence with the U.S. Coast Guard. As a result, we occasionally had lunch at USCG Los Angeles/Long Beach base at Terminal Island. The salmon served on Fridays was especially good.

Based initially at Terminal Island, and now Alameda Island in northern California, a USCG MH-65 Dolphin rescue helicopter made practice landings atop buildings in downtown Los Angeles. I enjoyed watching the touch-and-goes of the aircraft from my 17th-floor office window. Unbeknownst to me, Duke told the pilot about my interest, and every time the copter practiced rooftop landings, the copter would hover momentarily in front of my window. I felt honored.

Government Contractor

During my second year as a Group Supervisor, I learned that an enforcement group at the LAFD used several government contractors who supported criminal cases by conducting financial investigations in support of asset forfeiture and provided money laundering expertise. In talking with them, I found I had all the qualifications, and there was an upcoming vacancy. Unfortunately, while a supervisor in intelligence, I missed the excitement of conducting financial and money laundering investigations, so I applied.

On October 31, 2017, I retired from the DEA. The next day I became a government contractor with a private company with a contract with the U.S. Department of Justice.

My official title was an SFI (Senior Financial Investigator) assigned to the DEA LAFD Orange County District Office. An SFI has a Top-Secret Clearance and works with law enforcement personnel from local, state, and federal law enforcement agencies and OCDETFs as subject matter experts on the financial aspects of an investigation. SFIs organize and conduct detailed examinations of information generated during complex financial, criminal, and civil investigations.

I was orientated to the position by former IRS Special Agent SFI Charles E. Mullaly, CFE. Chuck and I had much in common, including tenaciously going after targets involved in money laundering and researching history. We also worked on cases together.

During the next four years, I supported Diversion, Cyber, and drug trafficking investigations in Orange County.

DEA Diversion targets individuals who divert controlled substances, including pharmaceuticals, from their lawful purpose. My first case involved a physician who overprescribed oxycodone and other Schedule I & II drugs and profited from illegal sales. In addition, a pharmacy—the doctor sent patients to—was profiting from his illegal conduct. The doctor, who was in the midst of bankruptcy, wrote over 50,000 prescriptions in a short period. He used the profits on trips, luxury vehicles, and sports equipment. During this time, the pharmacist pocketed nearly a quarter of a million dollars from the distribution of oxycodone and other controlled substances.

In one of my drug trafficking investigations, I worked with SFI Mullaly assisting a task force in the Coachella Valley targeting methamphetamine distribution and money laundering. The traffickers handled hundreds of pounds of meth distributed to street dealers in Riverside County. In addition, hair salons laundered money through their bank accounts.

Over the last decade, the internet (cyber) has exacerbated controlled substances like heroin, cocaine, methamphetamine, and pharmaceutical substances such as oxycodone and fentanyl by becoming a marketplace. For example, criminals use the Dark Web to buy and sell various illegal products and services. For instance, illicitly manufactured fentanyl, in powder form, is ordered from a Dark Web site. The dealer then mixes it with cocaine or other drugs, presses it into pills, and then sold on the internet. In one case, I assisted in identifying a drug dealer and his customers who used the U.S. Postal Service and received fentanyl pills through the mail. Unfortunately, from the dealer's mailing list, seven customers were identified as overdosing on the fentanyl they received. Agents then added this information to the prosecution of the dealer.

I officially retired from my contractor position on December 31, 2021. My only regret was leaving all the great people I worked with in Orange County and in the Division. I did not miss the drives to Santa Ana and downtown Los Angeles from my home in South Orange County.

Epilogue

One sport I have yet to announce is boxing. One of the private security jobs I worked for Lou McClary was handling boxing great Mike Tyson's press conference. Seeing his physique up close—chest, shoulders, arms, and legs—he looked like a chiseled statue I had seen in Rome. I could not imagine wearing boxing gloves or entering a ring and facing a formidable opponent. The training boxers go through is foreboding.

I grew up in the era of some of the greatest boxers of all time, such as Mohammed Ali, Sonny Liston, and Sugar Ray Robinson.

I never thought I would own a pair of boxing gloves and learn to become a boxer. Then, on October 15, 2022, I was diagnosed with Parkinson's disease. I had no idea how I would fight Parkinson's. Then an acquaintance gave me the telephone number of a retired California Highway Patrolman battling Parkinson's by boxing. Peter Mader invited me to a Rock Steady Boxing session at The Donna Clervi Foundation, temporarily housed in Rancho Santa Margarita in Orange County, California. From 30-50 men and women with Parkinson's, ranging in age from their 40s through 90s, can attend sessions of 90-minute workouts on Mondays, Tuesdays, Wednesdays, and Fridays, usually from 10:30 am to 12:00 pm. Workouts consist of 30 minutes of stretching and exercises, 30 minutes of shadow and punching-bag drills, and 30 minutes of floor exercises. The coaching and training staff have a caring and encouraging demeanor that drives participants to go above and beyond their abilities. After my first session, my legs were so wobbly I could barely make it to my car.

The Donna Clervi Foundation is committed to building a Parkinson's Development Center in Orange County dedicated to people with Parkinson's, their families, and their support systems through The Parkinson's Development Center Project. The project will feature various forms of fitness, targeted therapy, and fun, all to support better the physical, social, and emotional health of the Parkinson's community.

Acknowledgments

I am very grateful to the many instructors, mentors, fellow partners, civilians, special agents, family members, acquaintances, and crooks who contributed to my development, confidence, and experiences on and off the sports field and streets.

About the Author

During a law enforcement career that spanned 48 years, Detective Dennis Packer led task forces targeting drug trafficking, money laundering, organized crime, and corruption by police officers. In his spare time, he introduced five presidents, Pope John Paul II, the Queen of England, and the license plates of cars that had their lights left on as the public address announcer for just about every professional and collegiate sports team in Southern California, Oakland, and San Diego. Married, a father of two, and two grandchildren, Dennis has led an entire life filled with exciting stories and humor.

Made in the USA
Las Vegas, NV
18 June 2024

91204456R00144